AXEL JANIEC & TRISTAN POETZSCH

HOW NOT TO SUCK AT CONSULTING

28 INSIGHTS AND TACTICS FOR EVERYBODY
STARTING IN THE CONSULTING INDUSTRY

IMPRESSUM

The content in this book is not related to any specific company, person or team in any way, shape or form. Names, characters, businesses, places, events, locales, and incidents are either the products of the authors' imagination or used in a fictitious manner. Any resemblance to actual persons, living or dead, or actual events is purely coincidental.
The content of this book is created on the basis of models, personal observations as well as interviews across the consulting industry. It has been consciously decided to not give personal information about our interviewees. Firstly because the content in the chapters cannot be assigned to single individuals since they are always a result of a combination of all the input available to the authors and would therefore give false credit. Secondly because content may falsely be associated with individuals resulting in misleading inferences to real situations or projects.

For the sake of readability we used "he", "him" or "his" as a means to refer to all genders.

ISBN: 9798646581335
Cover design by: Axel Janiec & Tristan Poetzsch
Independently published

TABLE OF CONTENTS

PREFACE

After both of us had started our full time professional career in the consulting industry, our paths crossed in the management of a multimillion dollar IT project. While working on that project, we soon realized that our different approaches on professional challenges and life in general as well as our different educational backgrounds actually create a productive dynamic. One day, during an especially productive coffee break, we discussed the performance of new colleagues on our projects and soon realized that those poor rookies struggled with the same things we did when we started out. That is when we asked ourselves: why not help out here? As a result, we decided to write this book packed with the most relevant tactics and insights for professional consultants.

As it makes for a more pleasant reading experience, we decided to write this book from the first-person perspective. Expect some colloquial language, too. We also decided to write as dense as possible - no academical ballyhoo. We consciously decided to use this form of writing, since it will more likely trigger your brain to relate to the content and therefore get it right through to you.

If you would take only one thing from this book, it should be how to take the first step towards not sucking as a consultant, which is: sucking as a consultant. Let me elaborate: taking the first step towards getting better is understanding what "better" means and therefore realizing what you are currently not doing in a good way. Let me make this more clear with an example: a colleague of mine who just started in consulting got the task to set up a budget report and, upon submitting his work, proudly boasted about all the colors he used. None of these colors helped in making a more valid prediction on how much money we would spend and it looked like a unicorn had puked all over the excel spreadsheet. The thing is: he did not have a clue what is relevant for making a useful calculation. But he thought it was great. Well, it wasn't. He didn't know what the relevant dimensions for a useful calculation were, and he didn't even know that he didn't know them. The key message is: you can only improve when you know that you have shortcomings. To put it bluntly: you must be capable of realizing that you suck.

Of course there is a (more or less) scientific model underlying here - the four stages of competency by Martin Broadwell. To summarize: the first stage is making mistakes without being aware of them. This is how we all start out, especially in consulting. To improve, we have to take the second stage and realize what we are doing wrong and how to fix that. When knowing about this, we can take on the third stage and consciously do things right. After a time, we will keep doing things right without thinking about it, therefore unconsciously making the right calls. This is the fourth and final stage. There are lots of blogs and books out there helping you take the third step: doing things right with the help of tools and techniques, but this book mainly targets taking the second stage and being conscious about where your blind spots may be in order to improve from there.

My goal is to make the most relevant lessons available to you and thereby giving you a head start into your journey. I structured these lessons into insights and tactics to clear things out for you. A tactic is a more practical skill that you can use more or less out of the box to improve your everyday work. An insight is something that you should understand on a more abstract level in order to develop the right mindset for being a successful consultant. But be prepared for practical stuff in the insights sections as well.

But how did I come up with all of the things in this book? Well, I talked to more than three dozens of consultants, managers and partners from all over the industry. In addition to these interviews I took personal observations, compiled good practices and combined them with scientific models. Subsequently I structured this book into four chapters. The first chapter "Steer Management correctly" gives you an insight into the position of management and helps you understand your own role in facilitating their decision making. The second chapter "Waste less time" helps you understand how you should spend your time at work. This includes the difference between being productive and being busy, not reinventing the wheel and focusing on progress instead of deliverables. The third chapter "Get good performance ratings" encompasses how to identify what the important rating characteristics in your company are and how you get into a mindset in which you automatically get good ratings. The last chapter "Make better decisions" helps you make conscious and informed decisions, steering others into your preferred direction and keeping productivity high even when exposed to change. As a good consultant you should not only state what is in scope, but also what is explicitly out of scope: this book does not include the hard skills you need as a consultant such as strategic frameworks, Excel or PowerPoint - you can google that stuff anyhow.

Before delving into the depths of what makes a good consultant, I wanted to just lay out some ground rules:

1. Every chapter stands for itself and can therefore be read without the context of the others. You can skip chapters and focus on the ones most relevant to you. You should pick a few learnings at a time and try to be conscious about how you may apply them before moving on. Picking up this book every once in a while may provide you with he best overall experience. A more overarching view on consulting will unfold once you have read all insights and tactics.

2. As with everything you read: take it with a grain of salt. Your own experience, projects and team situations may differ and therefore you should always critically reflect what you read.
3. This won't be easy. And at some point it will be substantially more about understanding people than it will be about understanding EBITDAs and discounted cash flows.

And now, without further ado, let's get down and dirty: taking the first step - suck at consulting!

CHAPTER 1: STEER MANAGEMENT CORRECTLY

You may ask yourself what this cryptic chapter may be about. Well, it is about the single most important skill you need to develop as a consultant - as well as the one most people can't really put into words. It is about the main goal of your job - helping upper management (your own and your clients') do their job well. Because this skill is so important it is the major one you develop during your first years and it will determine how successful you will be as a consultant.

To make this right, I will get you started with three insights: what your job and your managers' job actually are, why you shouldn't expect your manager to have all the answers and when it is the right time to address your issues with management. This will help you get a clear understanding of how to fill the role you are expected to embody. Then, you will learn five key tactics you need to master to live up to this role on a practical level: how to direct attention towards where you want it to go, how to manage expectations, how to communicate your approach, how to brief properly and how to write good mails as a consultant. Finally, you and me will reflect on what a win-win mindset is and why you should embrace it.

UNDERSTAND YOUR OWN JOB AND YOUR MANAGERS'

INSIGHT

To take the first steps in steering management you must first understand what your job is and what your manager's job is. A manager's main task is making decisions and being responsible for them. This is also why managers are paid significantly more than others - it is not about skills, it is rather about taking responsibility and the associated personal risks. But as your manager has more topics on his plate than he can handle alone, he needs someone to prepare decisions and procedures. This is where you come in. To be brief: your job is to help your manager be good at theirs and making the right decisions. You may have some specific tasks like modeling or analysis, but this is the surface work. To actually be good at your job, you need to do a lot of the legwork you may have initially thought to be your managers'. But what does this include? Well, it consists of four big areas:

1. **UNDERSTANDING TOPICS QUICKLY**

   Getting details and being able to repeat them on different levels of abstraction is your first order of business. Especially the last part is important, as different managers may not only need different levels of detail, but also different perspectives on a topic. For example, a CIO may need to know whether a specific technical solution is reliable from an IT point of view whereas a CFO needs information on the associated cost of the whole thing. If you want to improve here, practice explaining difficult stuff to other people, like your grandmother or a friend.

2. **UNDERSTANDING WHAT IS DEMANDED OF YOU AND PRODUCING FITTING DELIVERABLES WITH AS LITTLE GUIDANCE AS POSSIBLE**

   This is important because quickly grasping what someone wants from you and not needing a lot of loops with your manager to refine what should be the output is good for your health and your rating. If you want to improve here, you should try asking more questions directly upon receiving a task to refine the deliverables instantaneously.

3. **PREPARING DECISION OPTIONS AND SCENARIOS WITH PROS AND CONS**

   Coming up with different approaches and evaluating them is a very time-consuming task and needs a structured approach, but the real challenge is putting the right three options up for debate out of all the nuances and uncountable options. If you want to improve here, try writing up options on a flipchart frequently. Start with the recipe for an easy option, a long-term option and a politically balanced option.

4. **BEING ABLE TO ASK THE RIGHT QUESTIONS AND (EVEN MORE IMPORTANTLY) ACTUALLY LISTENING TO THE ANSWERS**

   Spotting flaws in planning, ideas, discussions and opening them up is a prerequisite to improving both the discussion culture as well as the results significantly. To improve here, try spotting good questions more consciously, which is easy if you know what reactions you are looking for: people either start to think loudly or look baffled upon hearing these. Sometimes people even get emotional because they have no answer.

After reading this job profile, you may see it coming: although your manager is calling the shots, you are the one steering the decisions and procedures by providing the right information at the right time, preparing the decision options and asking the right questions. Equipped with this insight, you just jump-started your learning process. And to give you an even bigger head start the following sections will give you some additional insights into how you can steer management correctly.

TO SUM THIS SECTION UP

You need to understand that your job is to set up managers to do their job and therefore steer their power and attention by providing concise analysis, background and decision options.

DON'T EXPECT YOUR MANAGER TO KNOW ALL THE ANSWERS

INSIGHT

Especially when starting a new project, there is a lot of yet undiscovered territory. The first two weeks often feel like a complete chaos with a lot of information and expectations coming from all kinds of directions. Just like when starting an expedition into the jungle you just can't be overprepared in order to anticipate all the creatures, plants and dangers you will encounter along your path. In quite a lot of cases you will not initially understand all the details - that is totally fine, either because you will understand them later or because they are simply not important. But if something in the overall project setup (e.g. customer expectations, timeline, scope etc.) does not seem right, you should investigate it. Do not assume that your manager planned everything the perfect way right from the start. In case you feel there is something generally wrong, you should address it right in the beginning (in a constructive way of course). Your manager will either be able to explain everything or you gave him the chance to reconsider and readjust things before it is too late.

I had to learn it the hard way: as a young consultant I was wondering why the timeline of a project was planned a certain way. I did not address my issues, thinking "Oh well, i am sure my managers have their reasons for doing it this way - I mean they have around 30+ more years of work experience than I do and they have done this at least a thousand times before". Guess what: this timeline later became the biggest issue of the project and almost led to its failure. Every time I thought "I do not need to address this question since I am sure management knows what they are doing", that exact question would have solved a lot of problems the projects faced at a later stage. Just because someone was assigned manager in charge of a project does not mean that he knows exactly how to do everything. Why is that possible? Here are two reasons besides the fact that they are just imperfect humans like you and me:

1. **ASSUMPTIONS WERE INCORRECT**

   Projects are often set up based on assumptions, since there are a lot of uncertainties about most parameters in early stages. By parameters I mean anything from timeline, methodology to scope. The best guess of your manager might have been wrong, even though it was to the best of his knowledge. Conditions change over time and even though your manager is very attentive and accurate he might not spot every single change within the project environment.

2. **INFORMATION IS NO LONGER AVAILABLE**

   As key players leave their positions, crucial information for the setup and steering of a project phase becomes unavailable. The person(s) who drafted the initial solution to a project may have been transferred from one department or company to another. Your manager may not be able to consult with them about specific information and therefore does not have all the relevant know-how.

As the number of hierarchy levels and team sizes increase, the feeling of "somebody will have thought about it" also increases. The problem is that everybody thinks that way. In order for your project to succeed, it is important to understand that your manager may not have thought it all through. By understanding this and therefore actively informing him about changes or doubt you not only do what you are paid for, but will also make your work easier in the long run. See yourself as a sparring partner instead of a subordinate. If your manager had all the answers to a project's challenges, your support would probably be superfluous.

TO SUM THIS SECTION UP

If something does not make sense or smells fishy to you address it politely and precisely. This way you can save everybody involved a lot of headaches and your team a lot of extra work.

ADDRESS YOUR ISSUES AT THE RIGHT TIME

INSIGHT

Everyday life in consulting is somewhat of a funfair. While your client's board meetings are more of a bumper car ride, IT projects are free fall towers and your lousy controlling attempt is more like a twister in overdrive, there is only one thrill ride that you really should be worried about: the carousel of nonsense that your manager is riding. If it spins too fast, it will definitely get out of hand and your engagement will go down in flames.

To put a little distance between you and this rather gruesome picture, let me explain what I mean by this carousel of nonsense. When you start out on a project, your manager will more or less enthusiastically take on all the topics that the client hands him - until they say stop. This stopping point is where they are already spinning the carousel of nonsense at a comfortable and manageable speed in their head. You may ask why he does that in the first place, but the answer won't satisfy you: it is human nature. You always want to create an environment with an optimal amount of activity - not getting bored, but also not getting overwhelmed. But the joke is on human nature, as project work will always keep burdening your project's agenda with new baloney and therefore spinning the carousel faster. And now you also contribute to the chaos with your questions, issues and problems. Congratulations, you are now one of the people that are pushing the carousel just a little faster and a little closer to catching fire.

"Well, that's the job" you might say - and you are right to a certain extent. Consulting is of course also about being stress resistant. But the thing is that stress will take its toll, even on your manager. And it will ultimately go how it always does - you will not create the impact that was expected of you because you got your hands full riding the carousel of nonsense in order to not get thrown off. But it is on you to avoid this. Remember that it is your job to ensure that your manager can do his - guaranteeing long term success and having the time to make good decisions. And another thing: trying to jump on a carousel that is spinning at the speed of a blender will end up in a bloody mess. Don't you do that.

Well, all this introduction and you still have not gotten the answer to the question in the title – let us do something about that. It will become clear to you how the answer needed all that introduction, because it is as simple as it is paradoxical: the best time to address your issue is when you have slowed down the carousel enough in order for your manager to have the time to deal with them. And this is one of the major points that differentiates a junior from a senior: understanding when and how to slow down. Be attentive, and when in doubt take charge and get something off your managers plate. Go and ask about your managers schedule and offer taking over something, writing up a briefing or preparing a slide. Do that every morning. Think about what the next five burning topics will be and get on them to prevent wildfires. And after you slowed down to a convenient speed, you can place your topic. And one little tip: when your manager sees you actively working for their schedule and not against it, they will be very open to also help you. In that regard - please don't think that "Is this a good time?" is a good question. You should instead always ask "When would be a good time to … ?" And when actually having clocked in your slot with your manager, take the following guidelines to heart:

- Control the impulse to ask everything instantly. Write that stuff down and wait for your turn.

- Take the time to combine several topics, don't come running every five minutes. Try to limit yourself to two slots per day.

- Be very clear on what you actually need. A decision? Advise? Or just for him to see that you actually get shit done?

TO SUM THIS SECTION UP

Slow down your manager and take things off his plate. Then put your delicious lobster of a topic on there.

DIRECT ATTENTION

TACTIC

"What a presumptuous headline" is what you probably thought. Let me lay down for you what I mean by "attention direction": attention is what separates you actually watching a movie from you "watching" a movie (doing housework or messaging friends at the same time). And just like you pay attention to various things, so does everybody else. And from your own experience, you know how fast your attention shifts when you are bored or the content is of no relevance for you. And in order for that not to happen to others while you are presenting your thoughts, you should be able to direct attention in a apt way. And yeah, you may see yourself as an everyday equivalent of a film director, just don't expect to be a Tarantino from the start.

But before you may start directing, you need to understand some of the basics of attention. Psychologists differentiate between attention, which is reactive (like you looking up if you hear a noise) and vigilance, which is willful direction of your focus on something. Whereas attention is very volatile and can switch several times within seconds, vigilance is much slower. And more importantly, vigilance is a depletable resource. Everytime attention is triggered by something happening in your surroundings, you need some of that vigilance resource to keep your focus on what you are doing. The best way to operate is getting into a flow state where your mind is focused so much that you become unaware of your surroundings and therefore do not deplete vigilance. But that is seldom the case, especially in a high-velocity job like management or consulting. So when you talk to people you want to convey your findings to, you actually want to generate this flow-like state for the people who are listening. Why? Because if you make it easy for people to follow your train of thought with their focus, you are appreciated for your ability to communicate in a target-specific way and you also have a higher probability of people actually listening to what you have to say and therefore act accordingly. Not convinced? Think of a time when somebody said something to you in such an overcomplicated or uninteresting way that you literally got a headache from that. After that, did you think of that person as more or less capable after the explanation? Bingo.

Moving on to the "direction" part of attention direction: in order to deplete as little vigilance as possible from your listeners, you need to understand and leverage attention. You need to provide enough triggers so that attention does the vigilance job, in the sense that your listeners keep being engaged in a focused way. But on the other hand you shouldn't overburden your audience with triggers, otherwise you are firing off a concert of focus shifts which in turn inhibits the ability to even think about what you are actually trying to say. How can you do that? The most common tactic in consulting use is storylining. This refers to creating an easy to follow narrative outline which you detail as necessary. The restrictions of the outline keep you from triggering too much undirected attention. That is the case if e.g. the connections between your messages are not clear and force your listener to make them up themselves (which in turn leads to triggering attention a lot through thinking). Coming back from these thought excursions needs a lot of vigilance, therefore you need to keep them to a minimum. This is especially important if you have a very high density of information you want to convey. But as there is a lot of great stuff about how to do storylining on the internet, I won't go into detail here.

At this point you may think "Thanks for nothing, why all the fuss about theoretical concepts and then not even a guide to storylining?" That is an absolutely valid question. Let me put it this way: understanding gravity makes you Newton, letting an apple drop makes you a dumbo. Understanding what actually makes people act the way they do will help you in many more ways than just applying a method like storylining. And to show you how attention direction is also relevant outside of storylining presentations I want to dive into two other important use cases. The first one is the art of nosediving: day-to-day talk with the people around you lacks directed attention most of the time. When you minimize how much vigilance other people need to follow your thoughts in daily communication, they also tend to like you more and are more likely to do things your way. So what is nosediving? It is the art of taking someone who is either completely unrelated to your topic (which you should always assume is everyone, even your project colleagues) or on the other side of the universe thought-wise and making them nosedive into your question or topic without the need for the other person to retrace your thinking process with a lot of effort. Example: start at a very high altitude ("You remember, we talked about process automation last week"), state your goal ("I just wanted to inform you", "I need a decision") and get down to your specific topic fast ("I found optimization potential in step 58b"). To round it off, you can give some background ("Everytime we sort a defect out of the production line, the robot takes an extra 5 seconds to adjust its position unnecessarily"). Always finish with the answer to the question "What do you need from me now?" ("I need you to decide: should I integrate the improvement in the production line?"). This may sound trivial, but a lot of young consultants approach their manager and start the same conversation with "The 58b potential, what should I do about that?" Try to consciously notice this and in response exercising the nosedive formula. The more you actively adhere to this, the better your impact on steering your management beyond meetings becomes.

The second relevant use case of attention direction is the master class: managing the vigilance level of different people in the room actively and simultaneously. You may need some people to be very awake even after an hour of discussion and others to better shut up as early as possible. This means you need some people to not deplete vigilance at all while others should deplete all of it as quickly as possible. This can be achieved by taking your topic into a direction that your preferred discussion partner is comfortable with and therefore can make connections quickly himself while the other one needs to familiarize himself with the topic all the time. Example: you want to propose cutting the budget for a lighthouse project. Therefore, you might want to focus on the financial performance KPIs and tiring out the CEO while keeping the CFO sharp. Or you match the individual attention preference of the CFO very narrowly with your presentation (maybe he likes information more or less dense than the CEO). You can get creative here and some tactics might work within some settings and others do not. The important thing is being aware of how attention direction works and that you should use it in order to become a better consultant

TO SUM THIS SECTION UP

You should be conscious about attention direction in order to not make people deplete their vigilance resources. This may be channeled for presentations through storylining or actively managing vigilance levels and in day-to-day-communication through mastering the nosedive.

BE CLEAR ABOUT YOUR APPROACH

TACTIC

In our daily consulting business management has to make a lot of project related decisions with the help of … you guessed it: you. Irrespective of the topic you will have a certain approach to what you are working on. To enable you, your colleagues and customers to reach your common goals, it is essential for everybody to know and understand the approach to the challenge. It doesn't matter if you are facing a one-day workshop or a five year IT project. The way you want to do it - including the tools, techniques as well as the modus operandi - have to be clear to everybody involved. In order to steer and empower management in an effective way your clarity on how you are doing things is vital. This might sound a bit abstract, but I will try to illustrate it with a few examples. Let's look at the importance of being precise about your approach from a chronological point of view:

IN THE BEGINNING: PICK YOUR APPROACH AND VALIDATE IT

One of the first things you should work on is a clear picture of the approach for the solution of the problem you are working on (literally and figuratively). If you are for instance hired to improve the quality of the management reporting in a company, it makes utter sense to define how you want to do it. To keep it simple, let's assume that you and your team have decided to reassess the key performance indicators currently used for steering. You have come up with the following three step approach for tackling this task:

- Identification of status quo of existing key performance indicators in the company

- Comparison with industry standards and good practices

- Identification and definition of relevant key performance indicators through workshops with management

The bottom line for making good decisions within the process of improving the management reporting is that everybody needs to know how you plan to achieve your objective. In order to ensure exactly that, you should inform all relevant stakeholders about your approach (e.g. the three steps above). In the beginning of a project you should start your meetings with this information. Your project approach should be easy to understand and visualization can help you get it across.

It is surprising how few people have a clear and presentable picture about their approach at the start. But why is it important for you to be precise about your approach right from the beginning? Because at this early stage it is a lot easier to adjust. Actively seek feedback on your approach. Ask the stakeholders if you forgot something or if they see a problem in your approach in their business field. This way you avoid fundamental logical pitfalls that will give you a lot of headache in the end. Looking at our example your project sponsor might tell you: "Step two will not serve our cause here, since our products differ highly from the industry standard and our competitors have a completely different operating model." In this case you can adjust the approach or discuss if it is worth looking into industry standards at all. You yourself might even have some thoughts on how to improve our exemplary approach here, and that's exactly the point. By involving the relevant stakeholders from the beginning your decisions will improve in terms of stakeholder commitment. You are creating solid, common ground where there is usually just thin air.

At the beginning it is a good idea to define an approach rather quickly - you can switch if the need arises, but don't get paralyzed by the decision on an approach. In the beginning it is all about challenging your first approach.

DURING THE EXECUTION: EXPLAIN YOUR APPROACH AND STICK TO IT

Once you have decided on an approach, you should stay committed to it. During execution it is all about keeping everyone informed about how you are tackling the challenge at hand. Explain your approach to every new team member and keep the picture of it in everyone's head. People will keep challenging your course of action, but here is the good news: 90% of comments and objections are crap (If you think that last statement was a bit too much, you should consider looking into "surgeon's law"). In a more difficult scenario your approach is challenged and it turns out that it is not suitable. Regroup and start over. Your common goal is to make good decisions. Since you conscientiously validated your idea of the modus operandi in the beginning and - as seen above - only roughly 10% of all objections are actually relevant to your approach at all, the odds are high that you do not have to completely start from scratch. First and foremost your mission during execution is to keep communicating a clear picture of your approach in order to enable good decision making.

Let's look at the following example which shows the importance of explaining the approach and sticking to it: management tries to improve their sales personnel's work life. A design thinking approach is chosen which includes working with personas and their pain points. A representative, fictive sales character is created and everybody tries to imagine that persona's main struggles in order to then think about how to best address them in a new organizational setup. After an hour into the workshop a senior HR-Manager says: "I think we should also include what our company is already doing good. I feel like we are focusing on the negative!"

At this point the approach needs to be explained and also why you chose it. It needs to be made clear that it has nothing to do with judging the organization but with creating a common understanding of how the sales organization should be in order to tackle the main pain points. If you would now start to also gather information about what's already good you will not meet your goal until the end of the workshop. In other words: stick to your guns if you want to be productive. If you let go of your approach, things will get pretty chaotic pretty soon.

Let me add a purely subjective observation at this point: senior management sometimes tends to think that their input should be in the form of objections. Particularly when they have not really contributed any relevant input up until a certain point of a project or workshop they will try to be "productive" by tackling the junior consultant's approach in an unjustified manner. The solution: explain your approach and stick to it.

AT THE END OF YOUR TASK OR PROJECT: COMMUNICATE THE APPROACH WHEN PRESENTING THE RESULTS

Give everybody thc chance to judge the task or project success based on the approach you chose. If you arrive at a mountaintop and someone up there asks you how long it took you to get there it is pretty pointless to tell him that it took you eight hours unless you tell him how you got there. It makes quite a difference if you hiked, took the ropeway or a helicopter.

If you have altered your approach during your project everybody loses the ability to judge whether you hit your goal or not. Decision Making becomes a lot harder when constantly changing the basis of judgement. That's why it is crucial to be clear about your course of action at all times.

To be more specific: when delivering your final results (as a document or a verbal presentation) make sure to not only explain where everything started and where you are now. Lay down your approach concisely. As management has a lot on their plates they might simply not remember how you tackled the problem, even though they were involved in picking and validating the approach.

TO SUM THIS SECTION UP

By being precise about your approach throughout a project you enable management and other stakeholders to make good decisions, pass informed judgement and thereby improve your project results.

MANAGE OTHER PEOPLE'S EXPECTATIONS

TACTIC

Have you ever encountered a situation where you put a lot of time into something and then still got a verbal beating because it somehow didn't match what was expected? Well, no need to explain the raison d'etre for this chapter any further. Failing to meet expectations is something that devalues the time you spent on your work and, more importantly, totally unnecessary. Clearing out the expectations before actually doing the work is therefore crucial.

There are three parts to expectation management I want to lay out for you. The first one is the most obvious one which is delivering expected results. Let's start with that. Delivering expected results itself has two dimensions, being the "What" and the "How". Both have to be clarified. The "What" encompasses the format and the content of your deliverable. To make it applicable for you, I have compiled a standard list of questions that you can use as a blueprint for clearing out deliverable expectations on the "What"-front:

QUESTION	POSSIBLE ANSWERS
Is a written document expected or just a verbal presentation? If a document is expected, should it be an Excel-Sheet or a PowerPoint?	"The deliverable should be a presentation" "Just give me the main points verbally"
How comprehensive/long should it be?	"Make it five slides"
What audience should it be tailored to? In which context will it be used or presented?	"The CFO requested it for a board meeting"
Should the deliverable be self-sufficient as a document and be readable without a narrator?	"The CFO wants to present it on his own, therefore it should be pretty self-explanatory"
What main messages should be conveyed?	"It should show how the cost per produced unit have gone up too much in the last months"
Which triggers should be avoided?	"Definitely don't bring up staff cuttings"

Once the "What" is clear, you should focus on getting the "How" straight. Does your manager want you to create slides based on his detailed sketches, craft the storyline live with you or just let you do your thing and throw you some keywords? When should the first draft be delivered, when is the final deliverable due? Are there mandatory check-ins with your manager or someone from the client before handing in? And remember: you don't have to comply with everything. Be clear about what is doable and what is not. This is also part of expectation management and separates inexperienced consultants from more experienced ones - always underpromise and then overdeliver, never the other way around! And to make that clear, your best work is definitely not done after 22:00 h. Plenty of others have tried and that is not the way to deliver great results that your customer will remember you for. And one last thing to wrap up the "How"-part: delivering in time almost always beats delivering in quality. Take this as your standard mode. And even though you might not always deliver up to your own standards, most managers and clients are much more aggrevated if you deliver late than if you deliver in time with a big fat "preliminary" sticker on some slides.

The second part of expectation management regards meetings. Being clear on what the agenda and the objectives of a meeting are makes you and every other participant waste less time and not be unhappy with results. This starts with giving your meeting a fitting and descriptive header like "Cost breakdown for project XY" instead of "Budgeting". Creating an agenda that has a clear goal as well as the relevant meeting points and sending it to everyone with at least four hours notice is also a good practice. When starting a meeting, you should always repeat the goal/agenda and then the timeline for the meeting. Bonus points go out for making out-of-scope-topics crystal clear. Best close out with getting the commitment from everyone in the meeting. Example of a good starting statement: "At the end of this meeting, I want to have identified all numbers that are relevant for our cost breakdown and have assigned responsibilities for all of them. We have a time window of an hour in order to do so. I don't want to discuss why we spent some amount on topic X, please refrain from those questions. Is everyone on board with that?"

The last part of expectation management regards questions that are posed during everyday work. Those can either be by your manager towards you or you asking someone else. One popular example of mislead expectation management is your manager asking you about something work related, but actually he really just has one question for you: "Do I need to act on this topic or can you handle this without me?". Of course, the actual words are quite different, e.g. "How is the report coming along?", or more subtle "Can you tell me about the numbers?". Try to somewhat ignore these questions and instead answer the question "Do I need to act on this, or can you handle this without me?". Bonus points for Gryffindor if you also give an indication on when you will have it done. You will be surprised how satisfied your manager will be with this answer and how few follow-up questions will come up. But why does this happen? The answer is that most people think they make it easier to answer if they pose a more specific question - although in reality it often leads to a massacre of follow-up questions. And sadly, most people are not even clear on what they actually want to know. Therefore it is up to you to try and understand with what motivation you are asked questions and reply in a way that satisfies this underlying motivation. And when raising questions yourself, it is up to you to gain clarity on your own information needs and then pose a question that closely aligns what you are asking and what you actually want to know. And when you not only ask clear questions but also define what kind of answer you expect, you have ascended to the master class of being effective. An example for a well-crafted question is this: "Have we validated our approach with everyone on the board? This is a Yes/No/Don't know question."

TO SUM THIS SECTION UP

Expectation management can be broken down into deliverable expectations, meeting expectations and question/answer expectations. Mastering these and overdelivering on them really makes you valuable and appreciated.

BRIEF SOMEBODY PROPERLY

TACTIC

At some point in every decent American spy movie, there will be a scene when a high-ranking official enters the war room and demands rapport on the situation. Guess what: your manager secretly is exactly like that. You will therefore find yourself in the position to brief somebody regarding a situation or a meeting quite frequently. Admittedly, it is rarely about national security but rather about equity security, but the requirements stay the same: your manager needs a lot of tailored information in a very short span of time hammered into their brain by - drumroll - you.

A lot of people in business come from a higher education background. From a communications point of view, this can stand in your way. There are crucial differences between the academical writing style we are all used to and writing decision memos. Let us stick with the spy movies: in a war room situation, the writing style of your bachelor's thesis is most likely not going to help the high ranking official to make a fast decision. The following table shows you the essence of the two different writing styles and gives a good understanding of what is needed when briefing someone in a written way.

ACADEMIC WRITING	WRITING FOR DECISION MAKERS
Focus on past	Focus on future
Written for experts with no responsibility to act	Written for generalists struggling with real problems
Detailed, proof-loaded	Essentials only, meaningful characterizations
Short on conclusions, with a tendency to summarize	Begins with conclusions and explores their implications

With that understanding of the difference between an academical and a practical approach on writing in mind, let us get more specific on how to brief somebody properly. We should start with understanding what parts a briefing can have. In short, these can be classified along the information you want your manager to have: "What to aim for", "What to say" and "What to know". Going on a deep dive, let's take a look at what these parts contain and how you should prepare them.

WHAT TO AIM FOR

The first thing in a briefing should always be the current state of affairs: is the situation rolling and you are already working or is a decision needed to go further? You may think that you should start with situational descriptions or details but defining whether you are self-responsibly in motion or rather awaiting instructions is the most crucial information for your manager. The second step is describing what the current objective is and what course of action to take. Try to find the right level of detail for your explanations. After describing your course of action, the third step would be talking about "whose arses to kick". Yeah, that's right. If necessary, get your manager to enforce the things that are needed for your plan to work. That is literally their job. But you have to direct the foot for the kick. Be concise about what needs to be done by whom and until when.

WHAT TO SAY

Another essential part of every briefing should outline what your manager is supposed to say in meetings, emails or conversations. This encompasses on one hand a list of topics with the respective talking points as well as prescribed wordings and terms. The list of topics should be concise, but with sufficient detail to ensure its being read and, more importantly, understood even without your accompanying audio overlay. Please don't just list keywords, although highlighting is advised. And of course, you should focus on nose diving into topics correctly for both your manager and your audience. Prescribing wordings and terms in the context of sensitive topics like layoffs, restructuring and strategy is also of utmost importance. Most of the time a company's management has a specific way of wording those things. You should not only comply with these wordings yourself but also make sure your manager does. Otherwise you may run into problems with labor unions, other stakeholders or controlling.

When the talking points and the prescription are defined, you prepared your manager well for a one-sided approach. But you know how it is: people will ask questions. And especially in more critical meetings, you should be prepared for them. There is nothing more deadly for you than a manager stumbling through client questions, catching twenty tasks along the way and subsequently loading them off at your desk. Therefore preparation in this respect really saves you time in the long run! How to do that, you might ask? Try to imagine potential questions up front and maybe get someone to spar with you in order to get the right perspective. You can also read up on methodology to do so under the term "advocatus diaboli" or "devil's advocate" . As regards the documentation of these answers: provide them in a FAQ-style so your manager can react to upcoming questions like a pro.

WHAT TO KNOW

Well, you can be perfectly prepared for a meeting and still crumble under a question that only mildly goes beyond your reach. Example? How nice of you to have laid out your plan for the new AI system, but how will it accommodate the expenditure freeze from last week? Bam, you're out. You are there to prepare your manager for those kinds of throw-ins. You may ask how this differs from the "preparing questions" part from above. Well, this is more about general context with respect to your client and not about answering specific questions regarding your briefing. Try to relate the situation you are briefing on to your client's general current situation: what is their current strategy? What other topics are currently relevant for your client and how do they relate to your topic? What is the financial situation like? Preparing this kind of background context will bring the cavalry to your clients' rescue when they need it.

And of course, the hard facts and strategy papers in a company only make up so much of the decisions. An even bigger part is depending on the stakeholders, their power levels and personal interests. Therefore you should also practice your profiling skills - you will need them later on in your career. Start with compiling who is present in a meeting and what their respective agendas are. You can use the following exemplary template for a simple stakeholder profile:

Name	Stefan
Role	Head of controlling
What is his main goal?	Reduce fixed costs
What makes him look good?	To show actual cost savings in his monthly board roundup
How does he look at your current project?	AI initiatives are not worth their money in his eyes, therefore sceptical
Who influences him?	Stephanie, his closest advisor
Jan, the head of process engineering	
Whom does he influence?	Mostly the CFO
What are his current strategic initiatives?	Reducing CapEx by leasing machines

A briefing will most likely not help sway stakeholders who are skeptical or even against your engagement. Therefore, you should always try to win over as many relevant people as possible beforehand. And one last thing: as most people are not amused when they see profilings (especially if they find a profile of themselves they do not like), you should be very careful about these profiles. Keep them internal and only share them if absolutely necessary!

After you have now understood all relevant parts of a briefing, I must break sad news to you: It is not that simple and I am pretty sure you cannot apply this recipe all the time. Based on the situation, your briefing will focus on certain points, completely leave out others and will generally differ based on the amount of time and/or space you are given to actually do the briefing. Thus always be sure to understand your window of time for a briefing before preparing everything described above. Only got 5 minutes in a break? Or maybe a shared 30-minute commute to a client location? Tailor towards the time frame and your managers priorities.

TO SUM THIS SECTION UP

A briefing might encompass up to three main parts: 1) What to aim for including if a decision is necessary, the current objective and course of action and what tasks need to be assigned. 2) What to say including the talking points, prescribed wordings and potential questions. 3) What to know including general context of your client's situation and profiling stakeholders.

WRITE MAILS SO THAT MANAGEMENT WILL REACT

TACTIC

As consulting is a job you need a lot of information, coordination and decisions in a high frequency for, you need to have terminator-level skills to ensure mastering all of these. And at the core of this skill is writing sharp emails that get answered immediately. This is why I included this practical section in this otherwise more strategic chapter.

You can google "how to write a good email" and find a lot of valuable advice there. Most of it echoes keeping it short, being concise and proofreading. And while all of these are valid points, the consultant's lesson goes a little more in depth and focusses on crafting emails that will generate quick answers. Most managers only have so much time per day to spent on their mails and thus your topic. Cutting the needed effort for answering your mail in the overflowing inbox is therefore crucial if you want quick decisions. For this reason, you have to be concise. But the real secret is creating emails that get answered immediately. Here is how: go for full "decision item" in your subject. This means writing your question directly into the subject, preferably in a yes/no format. And while being as long as needed, keeping it short is important. Your main objective is the little popup window of you recipient's mail account (or the preview on a mobile client). When you press send, that little popup will appear and the receiver will likely read it. If you can successfully transport your whole information requirement in this window, you basically have an instant message which significantly increases the odds of a near real-time answer with the needed decision. Bad example subject: "Status change requests". Good example subject:

> "[Project XY] Can we submit the change request for project extension by 16/04/2018?"

You may have also noticed two little quality-of-life improvements for the reader: a prefix gives an indication of what is talked about and makes nosediving a lot easier. My recommendation is putting your project in [] brackets. Additionally, a (due) date should be given in the example subject (16/04/2018). This gives the popup-reader an immediate understanding of how critical your decision is. In general, there are only four kinds of mail subjects. Try to stick to them.

> [...] Input required by dd/mm/yyyy: …
>
> [...] Decision required by dd/mm/yyyy:...
> [...] Should topic X be handled like this?
>
> [...] FYI: ...

And here is also a guide on how to remind people of tasks:

> Initial subject: [Project XY] Input required by 16/04/2018: Cost estimation in 2020
>
> First Reminder: [Project XY] Friendly reminder - Input required by 16/04/2018: Cost estimation 2020
>
> Second reminder: [Project XY] Action required - Input required by 16/04/2018: Cost estimation 2020

So much for subjects – let's move on to the actual mail content. Best practice is leading with the central information requirement and the criticality. After this, you may show options for dealing with the specific situation. Clearly state what your needed input or decision is, define the target format and what the deadline is. End with background information. And one last tip for crafting a mail text: although you want to be concise, do not try to write bullet-point style or put every sentence in a new paragraph. One or two paragraphs should be your silver bullet for creating a pleasant reading experience.

As to the topic of highlighting: in a single mail, a maximum of six information elements should be highlighted. This also holds true for slides. And the highlighting should not be on keywords, but on implications. You can take the following guiding question to improve your highlighting: if someone just read the highlighted parts, would the relevant message be conveyed? This will become clearer by taking a look at an exemplary sentence with both good and bad highlighting. Imagine yourself currently consulting in the process of buying a company and the timing of the acquisition being key to the buying decision:

> Wrong: The **acquisition of the company** at a **target value of 365 Mio. EUR** can be done by October 15th if the antitrust authorities greenlight by August 10th.
>
> Right: The **acquisition** of the company at a target value of 365 Mio. EUR can be **done by October 15th if** the **antitrust authorities greenlight by August 10th.**

Now get out there and write killer mails with killer subjects.

TO SUM THIS SECTION UP

Write good mail subjects that make the decision options clear and fit into a popup. Structure contents including criticality, options, decision need, background information. Highlight not keywords but implications.

THINK WIN-WIN

INSIGHT

In a lot of cases you can witness people taking over a task or project, observing them verbally bashing their predecessors's actions and results. This is what I would call a win-lose mind-set - making other people's work look bad, so that mine looks good. Another common behavioral scheme is people taking on opposing positions (ranging from arguing about who's project approach is right to trying to completely stop each other's work). As a consultant, you will be facing a lot of these patterns of behavior. You might find yourself in situations where it seems that one party has to lose in order for the other to win. If we want to establish a trustful relationship with management (or any other project stakeholder), it might be necessary to look at our mindset regarding our business interactions. If you want to get what you want from management not just momentarily but also in the long run, you should consider embracing a win-win mindset.

Most people's default mindset is "win-lose". This is the mind-set causing the behaviors mentioned above. In brief, the underlying belief is: for you to win, someone else must lose. In game theory the strictest version of such a system is called a zero-sum game. In this setup the winner can only gain exactly as much as the loser is losing. There are quite a lot of reasons for people to have such a mindset – in business as well as in life in general. To name just three examples:

1. **UPBRINGING IN AN ENVIRONMENT WITH VERY LIMITED RESOURCES**

   If you have 38 siblings and there was only one loaf of bread for dinner you physically embraced the concept of win-lose.

2. **EDUCATIONAL SYSTEM**

   Quite a lot of schools and universities put competition before collaboration. Most teachers and professors are only willing to give a certain number of A's. I recall teachers saying "This would have been an A but since the distribution of grades has to fit into the bell curve and I already gave to many A's this term I will have to give you a B." I would call this an unnecessary creation of artificial "A-scarcity" supporting a win-lose mindset.

3. **MESSAGES IN MAINSTREAM MEDIA**

   A lot of TV formats promote a "the winner takes it all" message. Watching casting or game shows, the message you receive is always: where there is a winner, there must be a loser.

Get rid of the win-lose mindset. If you want to establish healthy relationships in business, think about them as a co-operative game - a non-zero-sum game. In this situation the aggregated gains and losses of the players can be greater than zero, hence everyone can win. For your consulting life this implies not fighting about scarce resources, but instead creating an environment granting plenty them: do not split the cake, bake another one!

Taking it one step further, it's important to not just make others the victims of your gain - the next level would be enabling them to win while you win. For example: if you wanted to increase the number of FTEs in a department, that does not necessarily mean that you must get them from another department.

The approach should be to enable the creation of completely new positions. Let's get a little more specific here: imagine your task is to establish a new software innovation department. That must not necessarily become a threat to the existing IT-Department. You can set it up in in a way that allows the existing department to do more being provided with additional systems to support and maintain. The IT Department might consequently grow instead of shrink. It's a question of mindset and the resulting framing of your approach. If you think it all the way through, a win-win mindset requires you to know the other's agenda. In order to create wins for them, it is crucial to know what a win represents in their point of view. A good technique is to simply ask your stakeholders: "What do you want to achieve here?"

Since not everyone and not every organization realizes what it means to have a win-win mindset, it is helpful to consciously choose where and when to lose. Sometimes people need to win in a win-lose scenario either in pursuit of their ego or political standing. In order to be able to work with these people in the future, you need to find your balance. Ask yourself:

- What is strategically important to me? Truly fight for that even in a win-lose situation.
- Is it worth the fight? Do not take win-win too literally. It does not mean that you have to win all the time. Choose your battles wisely since energy is limited.
- Does the other one need the win? If something is not that important (you might not really care about the name for the new department) you sometimes might have to put on a show and pretend to fight for a cause to enable you to grant someone else the "win".

Do not get me wrong here – sometimes win-lose scenarios are inevitable (e.g. cost cutting projects or negotiations about scarce resources) and it may be necessary to make someone lose. The point is: do not make others lose unless you decide to do so. Do not make someone lose just because you assume it's the name of the game. If your default mindset is win-win, you automatically expand your horizon and can identify more solution options to a challenge. By the way: you just learned about one of the essentials in game theory and behavioral economics.

TO SUM THIS SECTION UP

If people realize that you are also working towards them winning, they will be more prone to give you what you want and cooperate on the long run. Create a win-win mindset on a subconscious level. A consultant should always embrace business as a non-zero-sum game.

SUMMARY OF SUMMARIES

CHAPTER 1: STEER MANAGEMENT CORRECTLY

1. **UNDERSTAND YOUR OWN JOB AND YOUR MANAGERS'**

   You need to understand that your job is to set up managers to do their job and therefore steer their power and attention by providing concise analysis, background and decision options.

2. **DON'T EXPECT YOUR MANAGER TO KNOW ALL THE ANSWERS**

   If something does not make sense or smells fishy to you address it politely and precisely. This way you can save everybody involved a lot of headaches and your team a lot of extra work.

3. **ADDRESS YOUR ISSUES AT THE RIGHT TIME**

   Slow down your manager and take things off his plate. Then put your delicious lobster of a topic on there.

4. **DIRECT ATTENTION**

   You should be conscious about attention direction in order to not make people deplete their vigilance resources. This may be channeled for presentations through storylining or actively managing vigilance levels and in day-to-day-communication through mastering the nosedive.

5. **BE CLEAR ABOUT YOUR APPROACH**

By being precise about your approach throughout a project you enable management and other stakeholders to make good decisions, pass informed judgement and thereby improve your project results.

6. **MANAGE OTHER PEOPLE'S EXPECTATIONS**

Expectation management can be broken down into deliverable expectations, meeting expectations and question/answer expectations. Mastering these and overdelivering on them really makes you valuable and appreciated.

7. **BRIEF SOMEBODY PROPER**

A briefing might encompass up to three main parts: 1) What to aim for including if a decision is necessary, the current objective and course of action and what tasks need to be assigned. 2) What to say including the talking points, prescribed wordings and potential questions. 3) What to know including general context of your client's situation and profiling stakeholders.

8. **WRITE MAILS SO THAT MANAGEMENT WILL REACT**

Write good mail subjects that make the decision options clear and fit into a popup. Structure contents including criticality, options, decision need, background information. Highlight not keywords but implications.

9. **THINK WIN-WIN**

If people realize that you are also working towards them winning, they will be more prone to give you what you want and cooperate on the long run. Create a win-win mindset on a subconscious level. A consultant should always embrace business as a non-zero-sum game.

CHAPTER 2: WASTE LESS TIME

As a consultant you charge a high daily rate, which means the client does expect a lot of value in return. But that does not mean you should work countless hours. You should rather try to focus your time and energy on what is expected: creating value. In the consulting world this sometimes mutates into putting in hour after hour but it doesn't have to be that way. And you can actually do a lot to reduce it.

To help you waste less time, I will start with two insights. Firstly, we want to touch upon the difference between being productive and being busy. Secondly, we want to discuss working hours with you – and about what's wrong with working overtime. Be bold enough to go home and reassess your daily work to cut useless work. Bearing this in mind you should take three further tactics to heart: How to say "no" to the client and to internal work, how not to reinvent the wheel every time you are doing something and how you can diminish lengthy decision procedures in the client's environment by leveraging key decision influencers. Those will help you to really get into overdrive regarding productivity, pumping out great results both in writing and reality. Finally, you will gather an understanding about focussing on real progress for your client instead of paper deliverables.

BE MORE PRODUCTIVE AND LESS BUSY

INSIGHT

Do you remember the first time you struggled to describe to someone how you passed the day? This is exactly the moment you understood the difference between being busy and being productive. Busy work is what spoils your day with irrelevant calls, meetings, mails and other itsy-bitsy things that don't complete the big picture. The catch is: you will never run out of busy work, because finding it is easy. Even more treacherous is the feeling that this busy work is actually meaningful and important. Let me illustrate this with the following two extreme examples, which are more common than one would think:

> During a calm project phase, a manager gives instructions to his team to find something to do. His explanation: "We have to look engaged so the client/boss/other team thinks we are making progress."

> At a crucial and stressful point in a project, you suggest your team leader gathers the team, takes a step back and thinks about what to do next. Your manager's response: "We need to keep going -otherwise we would be like a mouse in front of a snake - paralyzed and unable to move. If we don't speed things up, we will get eaten alive!"

In both cases, not only will something be done for the sake of… well anything, but the velocity of busy work will also be increased. This is based on the common human illusion that success is about going faster - but it's actually about going into the right direction. Let me give you an analogy: imagine driving down the highway to get to this concert you always wanted to go to. How would you go about that? Of course you would use your navigation system and not just put the pedal to the metal. So why would you do the contrary on the job? Within everyday project buzz we tend to simply go full throttle without planning out the route we should take.

The answer to the obvious "why though?" is both trivial and powerful, because it is ingrained in our nature: it is easier to keep your mind busy with solving simple or habitual tasks than to strategically think about the productivity of your task – That's the reason why we watch TV-shows for hours without questioning what we are doing - it is easier on the brain. Since this is not so hard to understand, there is a lot of help at hand to increase productivity, from simple to-do lists all the way to the Eisenhower-Matrix (categorizing to-dos into a 2x2 matrix of importance and urgency). But the thing is that these tools won't save you: don't mix up being efficient with being productive. It's not the fastest one on the soccer field who automatically scores.

After all this "why it doesn't work", let me switch to a more goal-oriented mode to reach our concert in due time. What exactly is productive work? Well, it's all the tasks that contribute significantly to achieving a result that will sustain for the next two through five years at least. In reverse: everything that will be irrelevant in four weeks time is definitively not productive. Yeah, wrap your head around that! Actually, focusing your time on the right things is one of the hardest tasks achievable. How do you actually get more productive? The answer is: take your time to do less but make it more meaningful. Ignore stuff. Tell people to get of your back. And here are five routines that can help you avoiding being busy instead of being productive:

1. Start your day with a clear goal on how you will promote something today which will still be relevant a year from now. Block some hours for yourself to work towards this aspiration.
2. Especially when finding yourself half an hour into a task with no end in sight, ask yourself: am I actually creating relevant results or am I just being busy for the sake of being busy?
3. Set a mid-day time at which you ask yourself "Am I just busy or am I productive?". Put an alarm on your phone. It takes you only a few seconds, but it will save you a lot of time for the important things because you can readjust your priorities for the rest of the day.
4. Ask yourself "Why is this relevant?" five times a day. Channel your inner child and "why" the shit out of people until they stop bothering you with busy work.
5. Define the way of working and communicating with your colleagues (what is worth a call, what is worth a meeting and what your do-not-disturb-times are).

On closing this chapter, I would like to finish with concluding remarks. In our 21st century world almost everyone has access to infinite information. Simply doing or knowing more doesn't warrant strategic advantages anymore. Everyone could simply do or know more. It's all about the ability to focus on less - but on the relevant topics. Condensing information is our most valuable skill as a human in this day and age.

TO SUM THIS SECTION UP

Try to take a deep breath and ask yourself: "Is it the right kind of task I am doing, or am I just trying to do the task before me right? Will this be relevant five years from now?" Be self-confident enough to stop an activity if it is not serving the purpose.

BE BOLD ENOUGH TO GO HOME

INSIGHT

Going home when your work is done seems to be extremely challenging to a lot of us. Have you ever faced times when you were idly watching time on the job go by until it would be socially acceptable to leave? I am not addressing situations in which work needs to be done even though you have already put in a full eight hours – what I am talking about is not calling it a day after nine hours of work and no unaccomplished tasks left. If you know what I am talking about, I am pretty sure you know the struggle connected with this dilemma. Leaving office after having completed work is not tough when working all by yourself – splitting from a team consisting of a majority of co-workers who compete in the game of "who can stay the longest" is a completely different story.

Spending unnecessary and non-chargeable hours on a project is probably the most discouraging thing to happen to a motivated and result driven person. Just imagine the following situation: as a young consultant you start your working day at 8 am at a clients'. You prioritize your tasks and work on them throughout the day in alignment with your project manager. Everything goes according to plan and you are even able to come up with an out of the box solution for a specific problem. At about 7:00 pm you happily realize that you have finished all of your tasks in the best way possible. You pack up your bags and drop by your manager's place to say goodbye. His reaction: "Oh, so you already want to leave? Are you working part time now? Consultants are the first to be there in the morning and the last ones to leave at night! If I were you, I would feel quite guilty leaving even though my colleagues are still working!" You will meet these people in the consulting industry more often than you would like. But why did these people turn out this way? Let us take a look at the three most frequent psychological patterns underlying their thinking:

Firstly, some people honestly believe in the doctrine that they have to work long hours and that only the one who works the longest actually deserves the paycheck. This dogmatic behavior is often rooted in the way someone has been socialized and the cultural background of their upbringing. You can recognize these people by sentences like "careers get made when a partner sees you at midnight in the office", but those times are over. Just compare how Henry Ford's tayloristic factory system performs versus Google's business model today.

Secondly, some people have to stick around for as long as possible because that is their only chance of being seen. Let me explain this: one way of being seen in an organization is through the quality of your contribution. In this case your clients, colleagues or your boss recognize you because of the impact you have on the business you are jointly trying to improve. But there are people that are simply not able to draw attention to themselves in that way. Those people try to be seen in the literal sense of the word "see". They come early and leave late in the hope of literally being seen by others. These people enjoy reputations like "Tom is always the last one leaving the office." This is their only chance of sticking out.

Thirdly, in some peoples' lives there is really nothing but work. This may sound sad, but some people are detached from reality having been in the rat race for too long. Especially in the consulting industry, you will find people with no real friends, no contact with their families and no other interests or hobbies (personal remark: watching a soccer match in the hotel lobby at night is not a hobby). In a nutshell: these people have no reason to leave the office because there is nothing waiting for them.

You don't have to measure up to these standards – be greater than that. Have a mindset that is committed to contributing value and never forget: business is just a big game, but the stakes in this game are as high as they can be when looking at working hours: You pay with your numbered amount of days on this planet. With this mindset you will find it easier to be bold enough to go home when your work is done. To be confident in doing this, take the following three advices to heart:

1. Set a goal for each working day and make it public. If you have reached the goal, be proud of your achievement and go home - even if you are challenged about it. Try not to get sucked into meaningless work. You committed to achieving something of value that you made clear.

2. Be bold when leaving. Do not try to justify why you are leaving at that time on that day. When your work is completed, simply leave. Do not promote the rat race.

3. When checking out with your manager, ask "Is there anything else that has to be done today?". That way you are aligned with your superior and show the willingness to help if anything is time-critical. On the other hand you also show that you will only keep working if it is really necessary.

To give you a closing thought on the topic: If you charge eight hours, but work twelve, you actually give the client a 50% discount on your work.

TO SUM THIS SECTION UP

Do not get into an arms race of everyone trying to work longer hours for no particular reason. The currency in which you want to contribute is value, not hours. Keep in mind: when talking about how many hours to put in a project, we are ultimately talking about the most valuable thing you have - your finite lifetime.

LEARN TO SAY NO

TACTIC

Being able to say no in the right situations is especially important in the consulting industry since we are often expected to have answers to everything and be available 24/7 (just slightly exaggerating here, but I think you get the point). Let's take a look at the crucial skill of saying no from two perspectives: in a client project scope and extensive internal work.

To prevent your client project scope from growing in a continuous and uncontrolled way (also referred to as scope creep), you need to learn to say no to a lot of people. For a consultant, there are two dimensions to the topic project scope and of course an internal perspective:

PROJECT SCOPE

If you are hired as a project manager, learn to keep the project scope within the defined boundaries (with the help of a precise requirements list in classical project management or with a refined backlog in an agile environment). This is the single most important advice I got from experienced project managers and consultants. Keeping your scope from uncontrolled expansion is the make or break issue in most projects. Avoiding scope creep can sometimes feel like swatting away bees from a cake on a summer day: you constantly have to keep saying no to stakeholders who try to add new requirements to your project. Of course you can't say no to everyone every time. But in order to keep on top of changes, you need a transparent change request process which allows you, management and the sponsor to actively steer the project scope.

To make your scope protection more understandable for others, you should create total transparency about what will be done within the agreed budget boundaries. Even if you are able to realize more scope for the same cost: it still needs to be made transparent to the project stakeholders. In project management, the term "gold plating" describes the addition of any feature that is not part of the original scope. The thing is: gold plating does not get you the gold medal, mainly because it adds more risks to the project and because stakeholders lose trust if they are not involved in scope changes. Instead of assuming that you should realize as many requirements as possible within the agreed budget, ask: "Dear decision makers, we have been more efficient in executing the project. We can either give back 100.000 € to the portfolio or we can realize requirement XYZ for that amount of money. Since it is a requirement important to our customers, we suggest to add it to the scope and compensate for the cost within the project budget. What is your decision?"

ENGAGEMENT SCOPE

As you control the scope of your project, it is equally important to control the scope of your own engagement. Some customers see you as an all-purpose instrument, since a lot of consultancies offer quite a wide variety of services. Moreover a lot of consultants simply do what they are told - even outside of agreed and paid engagement boundaries. Let's look at the following situation: your customer meets you for lunch and says: "I visited your company's website and found out that you also offer database implementation services. I know that we hired you for IT project management, but it would be great if you could also help me with this database issue I have." In this case you can of course have an initial meeting about the topic but you should see it as a sales meeting. The customer is requesting a different service - say no to simply doing it within the limits of your engagement, say yes to developing a new engagement from this lead.

EXTENSIVE INTERNAL WORK

Let us talk about extensive internal work next. In the consulting industry it is common to work on internal projects besides your client engagement (internal knowledge sharing, publishing white papers, analyzing markets, conducting benchmark studies, you name it…). We often take on internal tasks assuming that our colleagues know how busy we are, but that is hardly ever the case. Since you will usually be staffed on a project for 100% of your working hours, additional tasks will eventually end in multitasking. To cut it short: multitasking does not work. Choose quality over quantity. Save your own and your colleague's time by doing one task in an excellent manner instead of several ones in a mediocre way. Don't get me wrong: I am not suggesting you become a naysayer; if you actually have room to do internal projects, do them. But in a situation in which your project demands all of your focus and attention, be clear about it. Discuss it with your team and define priorities. Let everybody know that you are willing to do extra work but only as long as your main task (delivering excellent project work) is not negatively affected, because otherwise you are wasting time. A strong decision-making tool in the context of learning to say no is understanding the motives behind the instructions you get. Are the instructions pointed towards productivity or to just keeping you busy (see above)? If you don't understand the reason behind your task: ask! A strong why always beats an interesting what and will give you the answer to whether a task is worth your time or not.

I have heard the following statement quite a lot in this context: "He is still smiling - He must still have the capacity to do some extra work." Why does that strike a nerve with me? Because it implies that some internal task is more important than your emotional wellbeing. To be able to perform at a high level you must be emotionally fit. The one who smiles is doing something right, not wrong. If people do not understand that and put a task before your wellbeing, say "no" to the situation.

Keep in mind that you will not be promoted simply because you did everything you were told. It might actually cost you more time in your development if you do so. Sometimes saying "no" can be a much stronger promotional factor since it shows the ability to focus and the strength to identify and articulate your goals.

TO SUM THIS SECTION UP

A clear and justifiable "no" can save you a lot of time and keeps you focused on the important things - especially as a consultant.

DO NOT REINVENT THE WHEEL

TACTIC

On an engagement, time is often of the essence and therefore you have no time to do everything from scratch. This refers to your approach in a project, your management methods as well as producing documentation of any sort. And even if you have the time to do things from scratch, there are two important reasons why you should not: 1) your time is better spent on doing the work your client charged you with rather than on recreating the tenth project charta layout and 2) most of the tasks out there were already performed by someone smarter than you – so why should you spend the time to do it yourself again and not offer the best possible solution to your client which someone already came up with?

You may think "But this has not been done yet, because we now have an agile/transformative/disruptive/ approach that is totally new" – let me stop you right there. Most definitely someone has done that already. You were just too lazy to check who has or too excited about leaving your own footprint. To become a powerful consultant, you have to build up a tool box of whatever you can get your hands on: emails that are well written, methods your colleagues use, charts from your companies engagements (especially the ones you are not staffed on) and of course chart libraries from other consultancies (networking is key). To give you an impression, here is the ultimate list of things you should never ever create from scratch:

STANDARD REPORTS

Project charts, status updates, steering committee charts, change requests – those are the basics. Your company has some pre-formatted charts and so does your client. Try to get both and compile what fits your desired result best. I also recommend starting to collect finished reports from different clients and especially asking colleagues if you can have their standard reports to kick off your library.

APPROACHES FOR PROJECT MANAGING

It doesn't matter if you are alone on an engagement or have a team of fifty people - there are existing documents for scope definitions, project plans, kickoff-meetings, communication plans, regular meeting schedules, project end reports, requirements for engineering and everything else you have in every project. Search your consultancy's library for the standard project package (they have one, I guarantee) and build on that. Otherwise ask consultants/managers who have done project management before if you can take a look at their library - just be humble about it. And one important thing: project management is about a lot more than just documents. Try to get an experienced manager to coach you through your first project management position and if possible, build on their methods. Frameworks like PMI and Prince may also be helpful, but mostly your consultancy has its own style of project management that you should roll with.

CONTENT SLIDES

as the trend goes from purely chart-based consulting to a more hands on approach, the need for weeklong PowerPoint crafting is declining. Therefore you do not have all the time in the world to do charts. The key here is recycling - but in this case not standard layouts like the above mentioned, but specific content chart layouts. If you have to do a deck, it is best if you have a layout for every chart in mind that you can recycle from your library. This cuts your charting time in half most of the time. Side benefit: most of the time you can reuse text building blocks (which saves you a lot of time) - you just have to adjust them to the client-specific management speak.

TO SUM THIS SECTION UP

There are a lot of things you don't have to do from scratch. Save your valuable time and effort and build on that. And also ask everyone if you can have their results for later reference.

IDENTIFY KEY DECISION INFLUENCERS

TACTIC

Did you ever notice how much power a child can have over what gets cooked in a family, even though it seldom takes part in the actual cooking? This is what I call a key decision influencer - someone who significantly influences what gets done without having an actual role to play in the decision made by the cooking parent. Therefore, if you hypothetically would want to influence what gets cooked at your aunt's family dinner, it may be wise to get your little nephew on the same page.

With business it's the same. Discussing what gets cooked in a project without discussing it with key decision influencers will likely be very time-consuming due to multiple communication rounds and explanations. This is because most decision makers have one or more people in the background whom they rely upon when actually making decisions. If you do not work closely with them, you provoke multiple communication rounds between yourself, the decision maker and his confidants. Therefore making things happen at your client and wasting less time is directly connected to your ability to identify key decision makers.

There are two types of key decision influencers you have to be aware of: the crucial prompters and the talkative multiplicators. The first ones you can think of as a teleprompter for an anchor which provides the text and the decision for the client manager. The talkative multiplicator is not as blindly trusted, but will trigger a broader acceptance for you and the results you produce. Let us take a look at these two in more detail.

Looking at crucial prompters, the first question that comes to mind is why there even are people that are blindly trusted. The answer is quite easy: decision makers have a lot on their plate and only so many hours in the day. Therefore, they will naturally look for people to help them make decisions. This is the birthing pod for our crucial prompters. If their advice proved to be reliable in more than one case, most of them earn at least some degree of blind trust. And what they also earn is a position as a quality gate for decisions regarding their area. This is where they get important for you - storming the castle is much easier if you open the (quality) gates beforehand. Let me give you an example: in a particularly chaotic project, the sponsor had virtually no confidence in any numbers I gave him. This was until I found out why: a lower manager (and also ex-consultant) handled all the numbers for him and was such a trusted advisor that the sponsor simply ran all numbers through him first. The solution therefore was checking in with the lower manager first and then presenting all numbers together. This way, every single number was accepted without a second glance.

This example makes the real challenge quite clear: how do you identify these people? The easiest option is asking the decision maker: "Whom should I consult with on this topic before presenting you solutions?". As simple as it may sound, it gets the job done quite regularly. A more subtle approach is listening to who is mentioned frequently in meetings or calls. Chances are high they will lead you on the right track.

The next challenge is to convince crucial prompters to support your position. To do so, you have to read their minds: mostly, crucial prompters have an agenda of their own. As they are highly regarded, simple praise in front of their superiors usually won't do the trick. You can gain their trust through two ways: getting along with them personally (lunch, coffee, drinks, asking about the kids) should always be your first step. But try to not be aggressive or annoying. As you are not the only person smart enough to identify them, other people also take this route and therefore a crucial prompter usually has a lot of people swarming around with fake politeness. Try to be authentic and open about your ambitions - do not try to be sly or amateurly try manipulation with the neurolinguistic programming stuff you read last Tuesday. The second way is an open exploration of win-win-solutions you can both support (more on this in a later chapter). Being able to quickly identify and effectively leverage crucial prompters is one of the most highly appreciated skills of a consultant.

Moving on from the crucial prompters to the talkative multiplicators. They are simultaneously great allies as well as inconvenient disruptions. When you gain their favor either by logic or by personal sympathy they will start spreading your ideas and results within their larger networks which often goes far beyond the people that you think are relevant to you. This produces a generally broader acceptance by a lot of people and chances are high that this will find its way towards crucial prompters and even other decision makers. A crucial prompter does not necessarily have to be high up on the hierarchy ladder. The main characteristic is their big network as well as their ability to influence opinions.

In one project, a talkative multiplicator triggered a peer of my project sponsor to push in the direction that I intended. The result was an internal drive that I would not have been able to produce in a million years, as it came from within the organization. The second benefit of talkative multiplicators is that they occasionally produce random wins. A client's employee who was part of the project staff I managed was highly interconnected throughout the different departments and hierarchies at the client location. And although he frequently had to be put in his place during meetings, a positive relationship with him outside of meetings made him trigger a project extension and therefore a longer engagement with the client. But despite these positive aspects you also have to be a bit careful about what you tell these people as they tend to spread news rather quickly and sometimes annoy people. And a talkative multiplier annoying people with your ideas and results is rather counterproductive. The line here is fine and you have to sharpen your own ability to actively steer people in the vicinity of your engagement.

Last but not least, you need to understand that these types of influencers exist not only on the client side, but also within your consulting company. Most partners have confidants which they rely heavily upon and most engagement managers have their "resident consultants" they keep close because they fill the role of gatekeepers. Keep your eyes peeled and try to apply your understanding not only to the client side, but also to your own firm.

TO SUM THIS SECTION UP

Try to spot key decision influencers and win them over for your agenda. Both the crucial prompters and the talkative multiplicators need some attention, but it is definitely worth it as they will minimize friction losses and time-consuming coordination.

FOCUS ON PROGRESS INSTEAD OF DELIVERABLES

INSIGHT

Done is better than perfect, because perfect never gets done. Especially in a project driven business like we face in the consulting industry this phrase needs to be kept in mind. Looking at the magic triangle of project management (time, cost and quality), a project's focus often shifts away from time, since people are eager to meet quality standards and aim to be cost compliant in the day to day business. Perfecting deliverables is valued more than progressing in the given time. But as a consultant it is necessary to always keep in mind that you are only hired for a certain amount of time. In contrast to your colleagues working in the line organization this requires a different mindset.

This difference can be illustrated by comparing the work of a stereotype German manufacturing equipment engineer with the work of an agile software developer: they both have in common that they want to produce a satisfactory product. The difference lies in their general approach and the business context they are in:

- The German manufacturing equipment engineer contemplates and thinks about the perfect way of constructing a machine that lasts 100 years and then produces it with the highest precision possible. The benefit here is that this machine will work flawless for the next 100 years - just slightly exaggerating here.
- The agile software developer on the other side usually thinks of his work as an ongoing process that is never

> "finished". In agile software development an existing software is incrementally improved by adding and changing little fragments every few months.

Don't get me wrong here: it is not about the actual jobs they are doing. It is about the underlying mindset. It is about the different general approach. These two approaches to the level of immaculacy both have their right to exist. It simply depends on the business context in which they are being applied which one is to be preferred. As a consultant you mostly do not have the luxury to choose. At times it is hard to stick to the consultant's role, especially when you find yourself in the daily business of a long engagement. What may help is the awareness of the definite finiteness of your project. If your customer needed the mindset and approach of the manufacturing equipment engineer they would set up a new department in the line organization.

Let's look at it from a different angle: for a startup there is a war of philosophies on whether you need a business plan or not. The truth is: the plan itself is not worth the paper it is written on because it is more or less instantly outdated. But the process of writing it and the associated progress you make on defining the startup is what is actually valuable.

The quintessence here is: as a consultant in a constantly changing environment you are unlikely to be asked to build something from scratch that has to last for the next 100 years. To be more precise: it is not about creating documents that are 100 % perfect. It is more likely that you are required to improve an existing organizational structure, process, IT-System et cetera. Thinking about your job as helping to incrementally improve people's business will help you understand that your final deliverable does not have to solve all the challenges a customer is facing.

TO SUM THIS SECTION UP

As a consultant you should strive for progress for your client instead of perfection for your deliverable.

SUMMARY OF SUMMARIES

CHAPTER 2: WASTE LESS TIME

1. **BE MORE PRODUCTIVE AND LESS BUSY**

   Try to take a deep breath and ask yourself: "Is it the right kind of task I am doing, or am I just trying to do the task before me right? Will this be relevant five years from now?" Be self-confident enough to stop an activity if it is not serving the purpose.

2. **BE BOLD ENOUGH TO GO HOME**

   Do not get into an arms race of everyone trying to work longer hours for no particular reason. The currency in which you want to contribute is value, not hours. Keep in mind: when talking about how many hours to put in a project, we are ultimately talking about the most valuable thing you have - your finite lifetime.

3. **LEARN TO SAY NO**

   A clear and justifiable "no" can save you a lot of time and keeps you focused on the important things - especially as a consultant.

4. **DO NOT REINVENT THE WHEEL**

   There are a lot of things you don't have to do from scratch. Save your valuable time and effort and build on that. And also ask everyone if you can have their results for later reference.

5. IDENTIFY KEY DECISION INFLUENCERS

Try to spot key decision influencers and win them over for your agenda. Both the crucial prompters and the talkative multiplicators need some attention, but it is definitely worth it as they will minimize friction losses and time-consuming coordination.

6. FOCUS ON PROGRESS INSTEAD OF DELIVERABLES

As a consultant you should strive for progress for your client instead of perfection for your deliverable.

CHAPTER 3: GET GOOD PERFORMANCE RATINGS

As mentioned in the introduction of this book, you need to understand what "good" is in order to actively work towards getting "good". Most of the time this is defined by others - for example by your company's rating system. Knowing what is expected of you by your raters enables you to not only perform up to these standards, but also to crucially know what is not yet expected from you - this is where you can shine. Instead of playing catch-up with the performance standards, you win over people by performing beyond the expected. And that is the secret to the high ratings you want to achieve. But bear in mind that the basics are also where you can disappoint the most, so don't focus only on the fancy stuff.

From this logic you can already deduce that getting a good rating is more about understanding some basic lessons than it is about specific behaviors. Therefore, this chapter will start with two crucial insights - how your company's rating system is structured and why it is meaningless because your rating ultimately is not about you. After understanding this, you will read on how to position yourself successfully in your company. These three insights are more about you understanding how ratings work in general and how you can fit into the top-tier spots within and beyond them. Moving on in this chapter to how you can modify your behavior to get better ratings, the next part will give you insights on why you need to take responsibility and why you should never be the problem guy. Lastly, two tactics on asking winner-questions and not justifying yourself will round off this chapter and leave you with some solid advice.

Before starting into how you can get those juicy ratings, I want to stress two points. At the beginning of your journey, you may not instantaneously find the opportunity to show how you can outperform. It may even take a year for your moment to come. That is normal. Concentrate on not neglecting the basics. And another thing: with the best ratings come the highest expectations for the future. A top performance is a marathon, not a sprint. The higher you are regarded by others, the easier you can fall from grace. Don't try to move up there if you are not ready to continuously walk the extra mile for several years. Sometimes a good, but not excellent rating is way more healthy.

GRASP YOUR COMPANY'S RATING SYSTEM

INSIGHT

If your company is big enough, it will have a rating system implemented. This section will tell you a bit about how you should interpret it, where to play by its rules and where you may try to bend the rules a bit. If you work in a smaller company, the rating system may not be explicit. This makes it simultaneously easier and harder. It is easier because the only glass ceilings are within your managers head. Therefore they purely depend on their goodwill and your vector of performance and charms. And this is where it gets hard: Because you have no defined dimensions for your rating, it takes a lot more effort to show your score on these only implicit scales. But although the following section may not apply to you explicitly, chances are high the implicit scales applied to you consist of these factors.

Your rating system most likely encompasses quantitative goals like billable hours and account volume. These quantitative goals then feed into categorical ratings like "underperforming", "average", "good" or "exceptional". As this transition of quantitative values into rating categories has category thresholds, your first mission is to know about these. You may find that the highest quantitative ratings are not obtainable by simply charging eight hours everyday and ask yourself: "Why is this?" The answer mostly is: Because there has to be a way to rate consultants higher who work overtime and change an "or" for an "and". So to obtain this rating, the solution may be one of two ways: Either you talk to your engagement manager or client about charging additional hours (well, it goes without saying that you can only do this if you actually put in the extra hours as well as produce additional results that make the client happier) or you take on side work on other projects while keeping a 100% staffing on your "home project". The first one is of course the preferred route of action, but not always possible. Especially in a world with increasing fixed-price projects, you have to understand how your management calculates projects and how big their leeway is. The second solution is possible through knowing the right people and having worked out a bit of leeway at your "home project". Tip on the side: Be very transparent when planning this, as otherwise you might anger of the involved parties.

Mostly there is a qualitative rating next to the quantitative one, which consists of at least the gut feeling of your partner up to a full-on 360°-Feedback. Therefore your first step is to understand how qualitative ratings are given out in your firm: Who gives feedback based on what inputs or experiences? How is the rating structured? There may be rating dimensions like quality of work, ability to lead peers or self-sufficiency. Upon obtaining these, I would always try to talk to your raters about what they would see as an overperformance in these categories. Ask what is necessary to get an A. This blunt but honest question will give you a very clear understanding of what is expected and may even prompt your raters to evaluate what is important to them and tell you that. And because words spoken out loud tend to be more binding, you may also reference to these later.

One last tip: Most bigger companies have some kind of time borders for promotions. It gets significantly harder if you want to be promoted despite not meeting these criteria. This is where most of the ambitious consultants I know hit their head on the glass ceiling. Try to decide whether you want to shatter this ceiling and then walk on the shattered glass in the future - think about strategically placing your demands with your manager.

TO SUM THIS SECTION UP

In order to get good ratings, you need to understand the rating system of your firm. Try to grasp how quantitative and qualitative rating scales work and what you need to do in order to get the best ratings. Lastly, try to spot what is not yet expected of you and shine there.

REALIZE THAT IT'S NOT ONLY ABOUT YOU

INSIGHT

When you understand how your company rates its consultants and grades performance, you can move on to how to actually outperform: by not trying to perform within your rating system. This sounds pretty strange, so let me hand you the key to really deliver an outstanding performance.

People who get into consulting are inherently motivated to outperform others and get praised for it. Certainly the reward is also learning new things, seeing different clients and making money, but by our needs profile most of us are performance-driven. May it be to show ourselves how we can continuously master new challenges or just get adored for being the elite by others. We can't help it, because that is what we grew up with and what was hammered into our brains from childhood on. And because we are so accustomed to how performance is measured and appraised by our education system, most of us think that in a job, performance is similarly measured and appraised. But it is not. You don't get a good rating for handing in an extensive paper with lots of side notes and context anymore. Actually handing in large chunks of information and waiting for feedback is not appreciated at all, because you create work for others. And this leads us to the main point of this section: your performance is generally measured by the amount of work you create for others (negative) and the amount of work you get off other peoples' plates (positive). Therefore your performance is not about you, but about everyone else.

Delving deeper into this subject, there are three points I want to emphasize. The first one is that effort is not getting you anywhere. You don't get a participant certificate for the time you spent on something. Your manager is not a teacher who will give you a good rating "because you tried". Your results matter, period. Your efforts and your feeling of entitlement based on the time you put into something are thoroughly misplaced.

Secondly, you have to understand that nobody really cares about you. Especially when starting out in consulting, you are one of many that fight their own uphill battle. And everybody wants to perform within their rating system to the best of their ability and does not really care about you in your system. And this is not only true for you and your consultant peers, but also for your managers. Your raters are also rated, want to outperform others and get appraised. Now we get to the itchy point: perception and rating of your work by your manager is ultimately not measured in itself, but in how it influences the perception of your manager within their performance system. Put differently: the work you do has the objective of helping your manager look good in their rating system (and in front of clients). Your performance is measured in how good others look because of it. Your raters will always find a way to give you a good rating despite not fitting into the ratings categories if you convince them of your performance in helping them. One might conclude that you should leverage the raters, not the rating.

The third point is more on a meta-level because it is about understanding the reasoning behind performance systems and the game that is played here. Performance measurement systems are constructed by people who are pressured to objectify their ratings in a setting where everyone is pushing for their next promotion. The categories are therefore chosen and defined in ways that are broad enough to allow individual appraisal between the lines (and consecutive promotion) while also allowing to justify not promoting someone to the next level. The system in itself is a justification tool and a grand hoax. But that is not to your disadvantage, you just have to understand what game is really played. Ultimately it is not about being the fastest in a rat race, trying to win the given game that has no real price and no real stakes. Instead go out there and define real progress with your manager. Don't play the game, make the rules.

Concluding this section, I want to stress one important point of perspective: In order for you to get an exceptional rating, others will have to get a worse one. But your peers' ratings are outside your reach. Understand that and understand your managers ratings from this point of view. Please don't think that you should bash others in front of your manager - nobody likes backstabbing, especially not your partner who relies on a balanced team. That is never the way to the top.

TO SUM THIS SECTION UP

Performance ratings are not like in school - you are not rated based on your efforts, but rather your results. And results are good if they make your manager look good. They in turn will make you look good. And don't take performance measurement systems at face value, because they are primarily justification tools.

POSITION YOURSELF

INSIGHT

As pointed out earlier, getting a good rating has only so much to do with you and a lot with the person rating you. And to get the juicy ratings, you not only need to impress with the best results, but also with being the first choice. This is the sweet spot you want to position yourself in. And as you know as a consultant, positioning has a lot to do with the surroundings (especially in your team, but also within the firm).

To position yourself, you have two major paths to take: Becoming an expert on a subject or filling a specific role. A subject is the easier option, as you can get infinitely specific with what you focus on. Market entry studies for pharmaceutical radiomarkers in Southeast Asia? Connecting SAP into a docker-based IT-infrastructure for production industries? Go out there and be the number one. But don't worry, this may take some years. The important thing is that you try to see as much as possible and try to rotate your roles even if you are stuck on of the endless engagements your partner milks longer than it takes you to explain consulting to your grandmother.

To accelerate getting perceived as an expert, one very valuable hint is proactively searching and reading whitepapers, studies and offerings from other consultancies. Partners don't make the time to read these but are always happy if you keep an eye on the competitors. And one last piece of advice: If you want to be accepted in an expert community, you need to have an expert question at hand at all times. One that makes other experts recognize you as one of them. For most people they emerge naturally, but you can accelerate this and come up with one earlier. And don't be afraid to do so.

The roles are a little bit harder to fill as you cannot just claim them for yourself but have to convince other people grant you these roles. But being established within a role gives you a lot more freedom in the company as you may choose engagements more freely and be highly valued. In general, you may want to fill one of the five roles fixer, mediator, strategist, wizard or rainmaker. Let us take a more detailed look at these:

1. **THE FIXER**

   The fixer is the person you think of when things get out of hand and you need someone with a cool head and a razor-sharp focus on getting things done even if the whole world is shooting against it. To be a fixer, you should be very stress resistant, not afraid of putting in extra hours spontaneously and be able to deliver results by the end of the day.

2. **THE MEDIATOR**

   A mediator is someone you think of if you need someone to manage difficult situations between people, mostly between high-ranking sponsors. To be a mediator, you should focus on being a relaxing influence, having win-win-situations on top of your mind and not be afraid to shit in someone's oatmeal occasionally if things are too stuck.

3. **THE STRATEGIST**

   A strategist gets called when the big questions come up. Strategists make you see the world more clearly, and open up a path where there is none. They create great narratives and break up existing formations. To become a strategist, you need to have a vision of how business will be done tomorrow and at least a little splash of creativity for aiding in that. And they read a lot, especially outside of their home turf. Bonus advice: don't think everyone at a strategy consulting company is a strategist or that there are none outside of them. You meet some everywhere.

4. **THE WIZARD**

   The wizard makes stuff happen and you don't even know how. Wizards are superb networkers, therefore they know everything ahead of everyone else and in the face of a problem they leave the room with their phone in hand for 15 minutes just to return with a magic solution. To be a wizard, you need to be able to quickly connect with people, remember their roles and kids and be able to bend official processes until they nearly break.

5. **THE RAINMAKER**

   The rainmaker walks into a bar and comes out with two engagements. Seriously, these people make business more casually than you drink beer. They can make customers see value even when there is none. To be a rainmaker, you need to be able to have the perspective of both management-friendly buzzwords as well as lower level concrete examples. And you have to be persistent.

But all the roles in the world have no use if nobody knows about you. That is why visibility is a must for you. Your performance and contribution to the firm have to be well-known and it is not enough if you tell your partner about them - you need several high-ranking partners to know and promote you. The only way to get there is working on internal high-profile topics next to good project work. This does not include making a call once a year, but really being at the forefront of business and developing new products and topics of internal structure. But don't try to hard: quality takes time. Don't do everything at once, but rather make time and focus on delivering truly inspiring work.

My last recommendation is getting into the vicinity of aspiring managers and new partners - they will probably want to prove themselves and need reliable people to help them achieve this. And when you are reliable, they will lift you up with them. Try to spot these and get in their favor by supporting their agenda.

TO SUM THIS SECTION UP

You should try to position yourself firstly thematically and secondly with a role to brand yourself within your company as the number one in something. Focus on visibility with multiple partners. And try to get into the slipstream of aspiring A-list-managers and partners.

ACT LIKE A FREELANCER AND TAKE PERSONAL RESPONSIBILITY

INSIGHT

Consulting as a job is quite unique, as it differs from many regular jobs in a number of ways. I eventually realized that there is one feature really sticking out: the feeling of being a freelancer - even as an employee. If you embrace the fact that this feeling is inherent to our business, you can pave the way upwards from the beginning on. So let's boil it down to two main aspects of freelancing, taking personal responsibility for engagement success and developing an account (aka sales).

Taking responsibility for engagement success and truly progressing your clients agenda is what differentiates a consultant from all the employees of the company. A client does not buy you for a job profile, but for a result. And that is why they pay such a high daily rate. Especially in larger organizations, the "That's not in my job description" attitude is very common among employees and cripples a lot of initiatives. Be there and do what it takes to get the results.

When starting in the industry, you may feel like there has to be some higher authority looking out for your engagement success as well as your personal wellbeing - but there is actually none. Yes, you are working in a team and there is a network within your company that can contribute to your project, but in its core the consulting business is based on high-performance individuals. Your daily rate is mainly justified by your personal performance. Of course you can consult with your internal network about your approach. Especially when talking about frameworks or templates you can and should get help from within your firm, but you have to execute the tools yourself. The sooner you realize that taking ownership for a project's success is important, the sooner your performance (rating) will improve - even when you are a young consultant. That also includes assuming responsibility for failures and mistakes and working on fixing them. I am sorry to piss on your bonfire, but there is no one who will come and save you or fix your mistakes when the shit hits the fan - you will have to do it yourself.

Often this may all feel like a one man show, which can be both: great and frustrating - depending on the situation. The smaller an engagement is, the greater the sense of being on your own and the perceived responsibility. The art is to keep this sense of responsibility up even within a bigger team or in a longer project.

Let's put ourselves in the shoes of your customer: when will he focus on your company and when will he focus on you as a person? In most cases he will be focused on your company during the tendering phase and then again at the end of the project when wrapping things up. But during the engagement the focus shifts to you as a person (or team). The point is: your customer focuses on you for the biggest portion of the engagement time. When interacting with you on a daily basis he does not care under which logo you are employed. He needs to feel that you are going to make things work for him and that you take responsibility for the results you create in order for him to be satisfied with your service. If he is satisfied, your engagement manager and partner will be satisfied and thus you will get better ratings.

Moving on to the second part of the freelancing feeling, which is developing an account (aka sales). There is almost no other business in which you have to start customer acquisition as early in your career as in the consulting industry - unless you are working in sales, of course. In the words of the partners of a consultancy: "An ideal consultant looks for new projects himself and wins new customers without external motivation. In a best case scenario he basically takes care of his own staffing." It might sound a little harsh, but the main concern for your employer is to keep you working on projects for which customers are paying the highest possible amount of money. Across the consulting industry "utilization rate" is the single most important KPI when judging the performance of individuals. How much of the weekly/monthly/yearly working time you are working on a chargeable project is the main metric you are measured against. Is this a good thing? It really does not matter. It simply is that way in consultancies and when talking about good ratings it is essential to understand this mindset. If your superiors don't even have to look for new engagements for you, you are taking their main concern off their plates.

Consulting is a people's business and you are always selling yourself as a person. Even though clients look for certain skills on CVs the main driver for long term business relationships is interpersonal connection. If you work on establishing these relationships and think about new customers and engagements with a win-win mindset, you are paving the road for a fast career in consulting. The difference between a freelancer and an employee at a consultancy? From an individual perspective it is basically the feeling of job security. You get your salary even when sitting on the bench. Especially in smaller projects it can pretty much feel like you are a freelancer. This is the reason why a lot of consultants decide to become freelancers. It is as crucial for a career of a freelance consultant as it is for an employed one to embrace the fact that you constantly have to work on acquiring new engagements. Talking about career: don't start thinking about acquiring projects when you are just steps away from applying to become manager. Set the groundwork early on in your career and it will help you advance and accelerate it.

TO SUM IT UP:

In order to get good performance ratings and pave the road to consulting success, adopt the mindset of a freelancer. Take full responsibility for your engagement results and work on acquiring new business relationships.

DON'T BE THE PROBLEM GUY

INSIGHT

When confronted with obstacles, a lot of us feel the urge to immediately share the impending doom with our team and especially with the team lead. This reflex is generally not a bad thing, since raising attention for an issue is important. But in addition to simply sharing a problem with your colleagues I encourage you to add a personal note - add value by offering solutions or at least your opinion on the issue. Let us make this clearer in a little example everyone can understand: Imagine you find a rotten apple and do not know what to do with it. You can now go to your manager, put it on his desk and say "I found this rotten apple and since I do not know what to do with it, I will leave it here - oh and by the way: it smells really bad since it is very rotten!" How do you think that will make your manager feel? The other way of dealing with it would be: "I found a rotten apple. We have two options now: I can either toss it away or we can wait and hope that an apple tree grows out of it. I recommend the first option. Do you need some time to consider the options? Otherwise I will dispose of it today." The conclusion of this abstract situation is pretty clear: do not confront your manager with issues if you have not tried to think them through yourself. And to reiterate what we talked about in the above section: a manager is not an almighty god of knowledge. Deriving solution options is as much work for him as it is for you. But the difference is that his time is best spent on deciding, not on coming up with solutions. That is your job.

Perhaps your manager even thanks or praises you for constantly addressing problems but that tells you more about an appreciative leadership style than about the actual value of your input. Look at it this way: you can either be the one who only "delivers" problems or you can add value to the team by addressing issues but already having different options or plans at hand on how to possibly deal with them. To your manager and team members it will feel like you are a constructive colleague instead of somebody who just raises concerns. Do not let it get to the point when your manager tells you: "It does not help me if you always give me problems - I need you to give me solutions!"

There is another topic closely related to this, but in a different way: the doe eyed "What should I do now?" attitude. This emits an aura of helplessness, which in turn drives your manager crazy, because it shows you are not willing (or worse, not able) to come up with an idea on how to move on from here. That is a deadly position to be in, because you maneuver yourself into a vicious cycle you can't easily get out of. Once you have the stigma of "needs to be told how to do everything", you will evoke a micromanaging behavior from your manager. He will then look at everything you do very closely, inevitably spotting further mistakes, losing even more trust in your abilities and then further micromanage you. At this point you have created a toxic work environment for yourself. Congratulations! Go switch to a different engagement and do better next time.

One last hint for becoming the solutions guy instead of the problem guy: you don't need your manager's approval for everything. Start out and decide smaller things without asking for approval from your first day onward. If this works out in your favor and you earn trust to handle things, take on more responsibility. But this does not mean you shouldn't keep your manager in the loop on what you do. Always be transparent within your team!

TO SUM THIS SECTION UP

If you identify a problem, come up with a solution before talking to your manager about it. Your manager's job is deciding, not thinking of solutions. You should never ask "What should I do now?" either, because your manager will lose trust in your ability to solve things on your own. Lastly, you should take responsibility and not need approval for every decision you make. Become the solution guy and stop being the problem guy.

ASK THE "WINNER-QUESTIONS"

TACTIC

Getting into a new project is always like falling down a new rabbit hole: it is a new world full of wonders, following weird and unexplained rules. The good thing is that although they are not written down for you, most people are willing to tell you what is deemed good and, more importantly, what is not down this new rabbit hole. You just have to ask around, following the idea of exploring the rules of a new board game and asking the most important question of all: "How do I win here?"

Why is this pretty awkward question important? Well, because winning is directly connected to your client's perception of your ability to deliver and therefore your immediate value. In the best case scenario, you will get a precise and straightforward answer. If you do not get a clear answer to the question of how you can win at this account, the reason often is missing context. In that case it is a good idea to take a step back and identify that context together with your manager or sponsor. The winner question here is: "What is our/my mission?". If this question can be answered, it is relatively easy to derive the requirements for winning, but in a lot of cases you will not get a satisfying answer. If your manager can not exactly pinpoint your mission and your specific tasks, you should develop it together. If there is no manual (or mission statement) available, you can create it by asking your manager or sponsor the following questions in that specific order:

- Why are we here? What is the cause for the project and where do we want to be at the end of the project?

- How do we want to do it? Which processes and methods are we going to use?

- What do we need to do/create? What are our deliverables and what are my specific tasks in creating them?

Yes, you are right: this is the concept of the Golden Circle by Simon Sinek - and it is great. If you have answered the above questions, you have all the input needed for a proper project mission statement and you should be able to derive the answer to the question "How do I win here?". On a daily basis or in task specific cases you can break it down even further and ask "What is the priority of management in this situation?". Write down your mission statement and embrace the answer to the question on how to win. Actually, I always write down my mission on a big piece of paper and hang it up in the office in order to have it present every day. This not only helps you understand your role in the game, but will keep you productive instead of just busy.

Sometimes it is as simple as asking a question. You would be surprised how many people just start working on something without understanding the overall mission of a project and without knowing how to win. And this is where this question affects your rating - it gives a huge edge on understanding what you need to deliver to make people happy. The simple but effective tool of asking the winner questions does not only apply to your projects but also to your job in general. And one last hint: a common mistake is assuming that the rules of the latest rabbit hole apply to the new one also.

TO SUM THIS SECTION UP

Ask "How do I win here?" and pin the answer on your office wall. You can approximate the answer by asking "Why are we here?" "How do we want to do it?" and "What do we need to do?". You should do this every time you get assigned to a new project and it is also recommended to clarify this sometimes in your day-to-day work.

DON'T JUSTIFY YOURSELF

TACTIC

All of us at some point got into the situation when we started justifying ourselves in the work context - albeit for unfair feedback or a plain attack from someone with a different agenda. In this section, I want to help you understand why justification is exactly the wrong reaction, because if you start justifying yourself, you already lost. This simple idea is as powerful as it is hard to act upon in reality.

Let me start out with understanding where our burning need for justification comes from psychologically: if someone attacks your sense of self (be it friendly via feedback or aggressive as a challenge), your self-perception is threatened. But deep down, you like to keep your self-perception nice and clean and think of yourself as never making wrong decisions or even failing at something. This is your most important psychological need besides nourishment. And that is why it instantly itches you to react and justify, put into perspective or defend.

Before delving deeper into justification and reaction to critique, I need to differentiate between reacting to feedback and being actively challenged. The first one is the easier one, as there is mostly no harm meant. If someone gives you feedback, they usually want to help you. Take it, smile, say thank you and think about why you got this feedback. Most of the time, thinking about why you got the feedback is even more valuable than the feedback itself. But when you start justifying, you are actually giving the signal that you do not value the perspective or even say that the giving person is wrong. Think about it: In which situation have you revised feedback because someone explained the circumstances? Although justification is mostly done without the intent of devaluing the other person's opinion, it almost always gives this impression. Just try to be bigger than your ego.

Now getting into how to react to open challenge, I should elaborate more on the psychology of power. Upon being aggressed, you see not only your self-perception under attacked, but also your social status and your sense of power, which is the value that you think other people assign to you. When you get told that you did something wrong, you detect a threat to your power and see your perceived value diminishing. The irony here is that the justification leads to actually losing power, not the critique, because justifying always means that you accept the terms of the critique and accept that you are on the defense. You concede to the game the aggressor is playing and try to compete in it. Think of it like playing soccer on hillside - with you playing upwards. When you start defending, you are playing soccer, although the playing field is tilted against you. The trick in this metaphor is not even playing on that field, but rather picking up the ball (in this case the representation of attention in the room) and taking it with you to a playing field you feel comfortable in.

This is pretty abstract and may seem a little far from reality, but let me give you an easy example: When you are called out for being late, try to lead out of the situation with something like this: "I see your point about increased team productivity by being punctual and would add that we should focus on stricter timekeeping. If you like, I could start piloting it now." This way, you take full control of where the situation is developing and you actually came out of the situation without even saying sorry (more on that later). Notice the several rhetorical tricks that are used here:

Firstly, you give your opponent the feeling of a quick win although you obviously discredit the generalizability of the argument by saying "I see your point", but not "You are right".

Secondly, you take advantage of taking your opponent by surprise and direct the attention to somewhere you feel confident about “I see your point and I would add XYZ”. This is similar to picking up the ball and moving to a new playing field. Try to avoid “but”, as it makes you look as if you were building up fronts. Substitute with an “and” or an “while focussing on”.

Thirdly, by saying something like “If you like, I could start piloting it now” you put other people on the spot and look like the only productive person in the room. This gives you power, whereas justifying missing the bus makes you lose power.

Admittedly, when someone attacks your facts or numbers, the situation is more complicated, as it is much harder to tilt the room in this scenario. Therefore if you are not experienced in deflecting facts and throwing smoke grenades (which is an art of its own), try to look like the reasonable party. At first, try to validate the claim. If you have counterfacts or find a flaw in the attack, you can easily take the high ground. If you actually made a mistake, discredit the impact of the mistake “What would this number change?” If you can’t win via discrediting, it may be best to accept your loss in battle and take the homework “I will check this again”. The important part in this scenario is to still keep going after this and not get rendered paralyzed.

Having understood theses tactics we should now turn our attention to one little word with a lot of power - “Sorry”. It is the correct choice of words if you hurt someone unintentionally, but it is not to be inflated as a particle of speech as it becomes meaningless in the process. Let me give you an example: I tasked an analyst to do the layout for a presentation. When I feedbacked it, he said sorry for every mistake he did. It is important to understand: you don’t have to be sorry, because no one is suffering from what you did. Take it silently and do it better next time. His “sorry” was meaningless, because it was just lip service. Don’t do that.

Sidenote: saying sorry, especially in power-sensitive settings like SteerCos, is always a statement of submission. Be conscious about sending this signal and how it will shift power in the room.

One last thing: you may have heard the saying “offense is the best defense”, but it is not as easy as that because a straight up attack needs a power position, good arguments and an opponent's open flank. Most of the time, this strategy only produces scorched earth and not win-win-situations, therefore you should be careful about this way of reaction. But don't get me wrong, this is also a valid tactic.

TO SUM THIS SECTION UP

Be the silverback and don't submit to other people's attacks by justifying. Tilt the room in your favor and let your opponent struggle on your playing field. And when receiving feedback, just shut up.

SUMMARY OF SUMMARIES

CHAPTER 3: GET GOOD PERFORMANCE RATINGS

1. **GRASP YOUR COMPANY'S RATING SYSTEM**

   In order to get good ratings, you need to understand the rating system of your firm. Try to grasp how quantitative and qualitative rating scales work and what you need to do in order to get the best ratings. Lastly, try to spot what is not yet expected of you and shine there.

2. **REALIZE THAT IT'S NOT ONLY ABOUT YOU**

   Performance ratings are not like in school - you are not rated based on your efforts, but rather your results. And results are good if they make your manager look good. They in turn will make you look good. And don't take performance measurement systems at face value, because they are primarily justification tools.

3. **POSITION YOURSELF**

   You should try to position yourself firstly thematically and secondly with a role to brand yourself within your company as the number one in something. Focus on visibility with multiple partners. And try to get into the slipstream of aspiring A-list-managers and partners.

4. ACT LIKE A FREELANCER AND TAKE PERSONAL RESPONSIBILITY

In order to get good performance ratings and pave the road to consulting success, adopt the mindset of a freelancer. Take full responsibility for your engagement results and work on acquiring new business relationships.

5. DON'T BE THE PROBLEM GUY

If you identify a problem, come up with a solution before talking to your manager about it. Your manager's job is deciding, not thinking of solutions. You should never ask "What should I do now?" either, because your manager will lose trust in your ability to solve things on your own. Lastly, you should take responsibility and not need approval for every decision you make. Become the solution guy and stop being the problem guy.

6. ASK THE "WINNER-QUESTIONS"

Ask "How do I win here?" and pin the answer on your office wall. You can approximate the answer by asking "Why are we here?" "How do we want to do it?" and "What do we need to do?". You should do this every time you get assigned to a new project and it is also recommended to clarify this sometimes in your day-to-day work.

7. DON'T JUSTIFY YOURSELF

Be the silverback and don't submit to other people's attacks by justifying. Tilt the room in your favor and let your opponent struggle on your playing field. And when receiving feedback, just shut up.

CHAPTER 4: MAKE BETTER DECISIONS

Not only your little nephew is having a hard time deciding between vanilla and strawberry at the ice cream truck, but most people are constantly struggling with making decisions. This is one of the main reasons you get called in as a consultant. Even if it is not explicitly stated in your engagement's scope, your clients expect the decision making to be improved when you are around. Therefore your ability to make and facilitate good decisions is pretty important. But before you can start deciding, you always need to start with the basic questions: Are you even deciding the right thing? What do you actually want to achieve? What is your goal? Are you posing the right questions?

This chapter will give your brain a head start in making better decisions. In order to do that, we will start with three insights that will give you good guidance on what to consider before making or facilitating decisions. After embracing that changing systems are not very productive you will look at how to deal with the information need required for good decision making. You will then advance on how to deal with the future and learn that it is best to base decision making on scenarios in this context. After this enlightenment, things get a little closer to the actual decision. With two tactics you will be enabled to challenge the underlying belief system of your decision and to really develop the options of the decision. In the end, we will get a little more metaphysical and talk about the principle of resonating patterns and how this understanding from physics can help you in your day-to-day decision work.

Before I will delve into the specifics of making decisions on how to move forward and change things, I want to leave you with one key question: Do you even need to change anything?

Because the cost of constant little changes may not be worth the benefit. Which leads us to the first section: changing systems are not productive systems.

REALIZE THAT CHANGING SYSTEMS ARE NOT PRODUCTIVE

INSIGHT

As consultants, we aim to improve the decisions that are being made in an organization while we are there. That's what our clients pay us for and even though it might not have been explicitly stated in the engagement contract, it is always expected of us. While especially bigger organization have often incorporated change management departments into their organizational structures, change is a topic that is only being paid attention to after a decision has been taken. A "post decision topic" if you will. My plea here is: let's make the implications of change a pre decision topic.

When (advising on) deciding whether to initiate a project that induces change, keep in mind that changing systems are not productive system. When change is imposed on an organization, attention shifts from "running the business" to "changing the business". When making decisions, remember this book and realize that energy flows where attention goes. And since there is only a certain amount of energy available - you need to consciously decide where it is directed. Everytime you are changing something it will need time to adjust, and this time simply is not available for productivity. Energy is now not focused on the day to day business, but on adapting to the change. Oh and… No: Not going into detail about "post decision change management" here – buit rather emphasizing the awareness of the implications of changing parameters before deciding to do so. There is a lot of stuff worth changing, but you need to consider the cost and collateral damage it causes to changing it.

Whenever you are about to decide on something or advise on a decision, include the answer to the question "To what extent does this decision change the organization?". This will automatically trigger more detailed questions like e.g.: Do we need to reschedule the project plan? How much slower will the output of production be if we move in this direction? How long will it take for the department to be back on full speed? Let's get a little more specific here: whenever you change a department's controlling sheet, it will take the controllers time to adjust to it. This time is not spent productively. The first couple of times will not only take your colleagues longer to use the sheet but it might also be faulty. The question before introducing the sheet should be "How long will it take the controlling community to adjust to the new format and efficiently deliver high quality reports again?".

At this point, you might think that a change now and then keeps things fresh and can't possibly be such a problem. And you are right about that. But if you keep an organization under constant change, nothing ever gets done. Imagine rearranging some of your belongings in your apartment every day. After just a few weeks you will hardly find anything right away. You will need way more energy looking for stuff then you would, if you reallocated your possessions only every once in a while. I know this example might be a stretch since not every change can be compared to putting your material life upside down, but it gives you a good feeling of the required energy and the disorientation felt by people and organizations if changes are induced too frequently. What I want to get across here is that the sum of "little uncoordinated changes" adds up to a big mess. Imagen the CEO of a big company is deciding which IT projects to tackle in the next 3 years. Even though every project will affect the organization, he is not being informed about it, since the individual changes might seem "to too small to be mentioned". His decision is now not based on all the relevant information, simply because people neglected it or did not read this groundbreaking book. Even little changes are worth mentioning. Don´t cripple the organization by constantly changing "little things" if you could also do it at a later point in an orchestrated way.

In manufacturing companies with automated production processes it is a given that when you plan on changing something you have to take into account the machine set-up times - if you do not know what I am talking about, you were probably sick sometime during your first college semester. It is obvious in the context of automation to include the loss of productivity induced through a change into the decision making process. It should be the same for any other decision, even when no industrial robot is involved. If you (or the organization you are working for) decide to introduce a change you need to actually give it the time and room to adjust.

No matter how small the change may seem: be transparent about it in order to enable good decision making. Keep your customers' bigger goals in mind and advise them on the consequences of their decision.

TO SUM THIS SECTION UP

When advising management to take certain decisions, keep the resulting changes in mind and communicate them openly. Include the implications of change into your decision memos and thereby improve the decisions that are being made.

BE CONFIDENT ABOUT WHAT YOU DO NOT KNOW

INSIGHT

You have been waiting for it… and here it is: a inspirational quote to start this chapter: “The wise man knows he knows nothing.” This sentence can be attributed to Socrates and I will link it to modern day decision making in the consulting context. The main insight of this section is that you should not expect yourself to know everything, even though customer expectations often make you feel like you should. Understanding your own limits is crucial for improving decision making and this is both your and your customers’ goal.

In order to make good decisions, you need relevant information. The art is to identify which information is crucial for a decision, even if you are not an expert for a topic. To put it a little different: when making decisions, it is not necessary to know everything about the context (which is impossible anyways), it is necessary to identify the crucial information. Even if you are hired as an expert in a certain field, you will not be able to know everything since there are always specifics to every company that you just cannot anticipate. Especially in the beginning of a project it is important for you to be open about limited or missing information and explore its impact. If you ask yourself what I am talking about, let me elaborate: There are basically two categories in the context of missing information when talking about decision making:

"I don't know and it is not important"

"I don't know but it's crucially important"

Talk to experts in order to identify if details you are missing fall into the second and crucial category. Don't be afraid to seek advice from the customer side. Internal experts will be happy to share their knowledge with you... most of the time. Talking about time: don't let too much time go by before investigating delete the facts crucial to a decision. Six months after starting a project it might not give the best impression if you are beginning to gather basic information. Of course there will be cases in which information is simply not available. In that case, clearly communicate to the decision makers what you do not know. Even though it might feel like you are showing some weakness in doing so, everybody will appreciate your transparency and it will even be seen as a strength in the long run.

Let's look at a practical example to get a clearer picture of what I am talking about: imagine you are hired by a large corporation to bring one specific old software up to the latest technological standards. The project sponsor wants you to prepare a decision memo regarding the steps to be taken within 3 weeks. After two weeks, you have identified that one major task would be to upgrade the software's data format to the current industry standard. So far so good, but for a good decision to be made you are missing an information: Will the updated data format be compatible with other software in the company's software system? You think about the implication of the missing details and realize that you don't know them, but it is crucially important for the decision making since it has an effect on the whole software infrastructure. When talking to internal experts, nobody seems to be able to give you a clear answer. Steve, the internal system architect, tells you: "I guess the new data format could be compatible..." The due date for the decision memo has come and you actually only have one real option if you want to enable the project sponsor to make a good decision on what to do next: be confident on what you don't know. Tell the decision makers that the software's data format needs to be updated to be up to new technological standards. What is missing for you to give them a valid recommendation for action is the information about internal software data compatibility. You now have the chance to let them know what you need to find that out. "If we run a quick series of tests we should have an answer within the next four working days. This will cost us about 20.000 EUR but will make sure the undertaking is thought through", is how you could suggest to proceed. Do not simply make an assumption at such a point – in quite a lot of cases people work with assumptions in order to save some time or to appear like they know it all. That might actually save you some time and might even make you look more competent in the short run but it definitely downgrades the quality of the decision that has been taken. If you are missing crucial information for a decision, remember this book and be clear about it. Decision making will drastically improve as a nice side effect.

TO SUM THIS SECTION UP

Do not expect yourself to know everything, but be very clear about the information you need for making a good decision possible. Focus on gathering the crucial information and be transparent about what you do not know. Decision making will improve if you are very clear about the required information.

THINK IN FUTURE SCENARIOS

INSIGHT

The decisions that you make today will decide whether you will have to fight the Terminator in the foreseeable future or not. So how can you stop the robocalypse today? Well, I can not offer you an easy answer to this question, but maybe help you with getting into a mindset to find that answer yourself! In order to do that, let me elaborate on decisions in general a bit (don't worry, I will keep it short).

Until now, I have talked about decisions in a rather one-dimensional way. It is an either-or-decision and you have to choose one option and you basically stick to it until you either succeed or fail. But the thing is, reality is never that simple. As military quotes state: "No strategy survives first contact with the enemy". Most plans are not worth the paper they are written on, because they become worthless when the first thing changes (another quote: "Planning only substitutes randomness with error"). The value of planning is not in the result, but in the process. And that is what you should focus on: spending more time on actually thinking and planning and less time on specifying one easily falsifiable plan of action. And all of this is not only true for strategies and plans, but also for decisions. Decisions need to be a little more flexible in order to deal with reality. But at this point you may ask: How is it a decision if you do not really decide? And you would be totally right, so here we are talking about one of the major bridges in agile/disruptive/modern environments, which would be scenario planning.

As an introduction to scenario planning, I want to explore one crucial change of thinking with you: stop thinking in fixed numbers and start thinking in ranges. People have a totally unreasonable preference for making everything a defined number. Why commit to a sales target of one million? Does an actual of 980.000 really mean failing the target of the company (increasing revenue) or just failing a round one million as a number? Why is the target even one million and not 982.465? What is the difference this makes to business? Numbers like these are arbitrary. Instead, you should start thinking in meaningful ranges and in thresholds. What does it mean for a company to make less than 900.000 in sales revenue? What decisions should the company make then? What will be different when they earn between 900.000 and a million? Maybe they would like to reinvest the additional value. And what about when you earn more than a million? Scenarios like these help you identify meaningful ranges that imply different behaviors based on a factor that has an uncertainty (like all sales projections do). And since we are talking about projections: never ever commit yourself to one number when forecasting, always talk about ranges. The longer the projection is reaching into the future, the wider the ranges of possible outcomes should become. Split those ranges into a conservative (read pessimistic), a "neutral" and an optimistic scenario. And then tell your clients their decision options based on these scenarios!

Now you not only understand why ranges are so crucial, but you already got the introduction to scenario-based thinking. Scenario-based thinking turns the logic a bit upside down, because the action is not the primary decision, but you rather decide on relevant dimensions which differentiate scenarios. It may be that the relevant decision is monetary (like above), but you may decide to work with customer retention rates, market developments or product launches by competitors. And based on the specific scenario, you think about what you would do then.

Let me make this more tangible with a client example. A client wanted to centralize his >40 locations. The tricky part was: it was not clear how hard it would be to a) hire new people at the headquarters, b) get them up to the task and c) how much pushback he would receive from labor relations. Therefore we decided for a scenario-based approach. We started with consolidating five locations to the headquarters. Based on how the factors would turn out, we had a scenario for a fast centralization, a long-term consolidation and a scenario in which we had an intermediate step with regional competence centers. This way, the client was able to react much more flexible and was able to communicate to senior management a clear way forward even under changing circumstances with relative ease.

While we are at it, most scenario thinking approaches should also include an exit scenario. A lot of projects turn out to cost a lot more than expected and yield a lot less ROI. This is a real problem, especially in IT/digitalization projects. Most companies suffer from a massive sunk-cost fallacy. Therefore, you should define thresholds for your client which draw a line in the sand and clearly state when a project should be stopped altogether (or at least discussed again). For example, if you are preparing a decision for a new investment project, you should include an exit condition like "If the prototype reveals the initial estimate to be off by a factor of at least two, the project should be stopped".

After reading all of this, you may argue: this is too complex, I can't explain this to people, they just look at me confused. This goes against what you learned - which is making it as simple as possible and understandable for children and board members. This is a totally valid objection. You can get lost in the depths of scenarios and build hyper-complex decision trees that will still fail due to real life being real life. But you can also limit the complexity. Just as I advised you to give three options in a briefing, you should limit yourself to three scenarios. This keeps the complexity at bay.

Oh, and one last thing: always clearly state that the information and recommendations you are showing are based on assumptions. This might sound like a given when talking about and predicting the future, but it is worth being clear about what you know and what you don't. This way your clients will perceive you as being more reliable and it also has the nice side benefit of improving your own decision making.

TO SUM THIS SECTION UP

Think in scenarios. This includes defining what the relevant factors are that differentiate the three main scenarios and how you should act under those circumstances. Stop focusing on single numbers and think in meaningful ranges. Define a threshold for an exit scenario.

CHALLENGE UNDERLYING BELIEFS

TACTIC

As humans, we only have limited capacity to grasp and process all of reality. To deal with that reality, all of us have a mental representation of how we think the world as well as business works. This representation is highly subjective and rarely has anything to do with what is actually real. I hate to break it to you, but that is also true of you. As a result one of the core abilities of a good consultant is to make these beliefs visible, which enables you to challenge them. This is a crucial area to improve on when facilitating better decisions. Hence, when aiming to improve an organization's or client's decision making, I suggest to analyze existing belief systems from the following three different viewpoints:

1. Beliefs about cause and effect
2. Beliefs about available options
3. Beliefs about desirable results

In a first step try to learn about your counterpart's cause and effect logic. How do they think things are connected? How does the model of cause and effect look in your counterparts' head? If you think that this is nothing subjective - well that's just because you think that your cause and effect logic is universally valid. The truth is that causality is invisible. I'll give you an example: "Hard work leads to monetary success." This is nothing but a belief about a causal connection which can not be proven to be universally valid. Try to identify these doctrines in your project context in order to challenge them and thereby opening up new viewpoints on the potential results of certain actions.

In a next step, try to learn about the predominant beliefs about which options are available. I would like to introduce you to a model that can help you identify certain thought and belief patterns: the tetralemma. This logic has its origins in India and will help you challenge beliefs systematically in the context of decision making. The word Tetralemma is derived of the dilemma. A Dilemma is a situation in which you typically have to choose between two ("di") options which are at worst both not very desirable. This already is a belief system. In a business context organizations, teams and individuals quite often seem to be stuck in a dilemma situation where it seems as if there were only two options to choose. An example would be a company struggling with the decision about producing new software in an agile way or in a classical (waterfall) way, but let's get back to that later. As a consultant, you can enable your clients as well as your own team to make better decisions by challenging the underlying belief system in a nice and structured way. Who says that there are only the two options you are looking at? This is where the tetralemma comes in. It helps you break up a pattern of thinking that would have lead to a diminution of options. Instead of assuming that you can either do option A or option B you can ask if it is possible to do both or to not do either one. This way of looking at the present challenge will then open up the question if there is a completely different solution option which has nothing to do with option A or B. When finding yourself presented with a dilemma situation, pull out the tetralemma and you will set an impulse to challenge the current belief pattern. To make it a little more graphic:

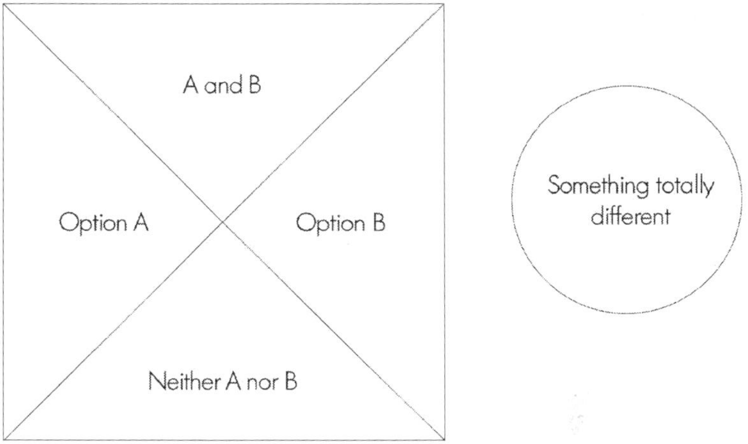

If we pick up the software production dilemma from above we can now offer more decision options. The company could do both, which would be a hybrid method of software production combining classical and agile approaches, like for example the "water-scrum-fall". A fourth option would be to not do either option. If the software development in your company is not really your core competence why do it yourself at all? How about buying standard software or outsource the software development? Or should we even consider the option of completely leaving the software market? If you identified the beliefs about the options available, you can now challenge them and thereby offer new options for action.

A third dimension from which to analyze beliefs is the way people think about desirable results. Decisions are measured by success - but success may not be defined in the same way by different organization and individuals. Therefore, you should ask "What is success?". Before deciding on something, it is of immeasurable value to really think long and hard about what a success is and what decision options may lead there in your specific context. If you dig deeper, a lot of times the definition of a success seems to be very vague. This is why most companies pay top people to break "success" down into a tangible target state. Let's look at an example before this gets too abstract: if success is defined as being able to react to changing markets in a fast way, the target state may be having switched all your software development to an agile method. But it could be that moving 10.000 people into an agile mindset is much more complicated than having a fast procurement process with an external software development company. What I am trying to say in this scenario: the underlying belief here is "We have to change our way of producing software in order to be successful." But if you focus on your definition of success that might simply not be necessary. It basically boils down to our understanding of the objectives of others. Do you really know what others want and need to achieve through this decision? A tactic on getting a grip on people's beliefs about desirable results is not only asking people about their own definition of success, but also about what they think their peers' definition of success is. You can ask "What do you think your colleagues are believing how success can be achieved?". The knowledge of people's beliefs about what a desirable outcome is will immensely help you facilitate the decision making process.

When talking about making better decisions, you have to understand the belief systems of the different stakeholders at your clients so you can systematically challenge them and align them to the common definition of success.

TO SUM THIS SECTION UP

Identify the existing belief systems within your project with regard to cause and effect, available options as well as desirable results in order to challenge them. This will improve decision making since you increase the options for actions, explore new business opportunities and therefore create greater impact.

REFLECT ON DECISION OPTIONS

TACTIC

Your day-to-day work as a consultant consists of preparing decisions for management most of the time. But just as the scale from white to black has millions of greys most questions in consulting offer immeasurable amounts of solution options. Which shades of grey do you pick out of this spectrum to present to management? Offering 50 shades of grey will obviously make them choke (alright, enough jokes).

The actual task in preparing decision options is that an infinitely complex world needs to be reduced in complexity to a manageable and decidable phenomenon. This section will therefore give you a practical guide on how to prepare decisions optimally for yourself or your management, starting with the general structure of preparing decision. First, you have to understand information needs for decisions. After this, you have to choose fitting decision options out of the spectrum. Finally, you must think of the consequences of the options you put on the table. But before we start, I want to make one thing clear: you are not in sales, you don't want to sell a solution. The best decision depends on the perspective you take. Therefore, as a consultant you don't recommend an option but rather a perspective.

And now let me start. To make decisions, the initial step is understanding what information or dimension is needed. What information do your stakeholders need? Especially for stakeholders, not all information is relevant. Hence, you first have to figure out what is relevant to whom in this specific decision context. In order to do that, you have to understand how they understand their business – both on a company and on a personal level. What goals do they follow based on this? What information do you and they think is needed to make the decision? This may include aspects like cost, expected benefit, effect on staff/ permanent payroll or worker council relationship, to name the most prominent ones. Make a list of the needed information, in a literal sense or in your head. But your ideas may very well differ from the ones your stakeholder has. This is because most of the time you are fighting against a predetermined solution path in your stakeholder's head. Most stakeholders reached their position by developing a highly functional decision template, which is their preset to analyze situations and make decisions, but you have to ask the question on what grounds this template applies to this specific situation. The often cited example of Kodak executives disregarding the trend of digital cameras as a relevant development is one of these occasions when decision templates failed. Try to make both available for the decision: what your stakeholders deem important and what you find useful as a decision basis. Trust your guts on the last one.

And one more complication: most of the time, you are not serving up a decision option to just one stakeholder, but to numerous ones. Here, you may encounter vastly different information needs. Let me make a typical investment decision as an example, because you are very likely to stumble upon them: the hardball optimizer CFO wants to see the monetary benefits on different time horizons (immediate, mid-term planning, long-term), while the strategists wants to know how the decision will impact the market share and possible expansion opportunities more than the immediate benefit. Know and serve both.

When you have understood what information and dimensions are relevant for the decision at hand, we get to the part you came here for: deriving decision options. But in order to obtain them, you need the decision criteria from our first step in order to understand where scenarios may differ. But instead of writing down these in some semi-structured way, I recommend using a morphological box to grid out different options. In this method, you write all the relevant dimensions in single rows and different parameter values in the cells. Then, you can vertically combine cells and see whether the whole option may be useful or nonsense. This way you can't overlook options. Let me give you an example: say you want to reduce costs per piece on a product line. Maybe relevant dimensions of this decision include how much money the board wants to spend on that initiative, whether a project organization is needed and whether it should buy or outsource parts of the production. Grid that up and now start combining the options until you find two or three scenarios that may be useful. Use this example and think some up yourself:

DIMENSION	OPTION 1	OPTION 2	OPTION 3	OPTION 4
Investment	None	200.000	500.000	1.000.000
Start optimization project	Full-scale	Small project	No project, let line organization handle it	
Buy/Make	Keep making everything	Buy some parts on the market	Buy everything, just assemble	Buy product white-label
Outsource	Outsource whole production	Outsource some easy parts	Keep everything local	

After thinking up options, start to narrow them down. As a rule of thumb, you can start out with defining a cheap solution, a technically best solution and a politically balanced solution (which is not necessarily a compromise between the other two, but something completely different). Try to make up three scenarios. Three is somewhat of a magic number for choices, as surprisingly many psychological studies conclude.

When you have your three picks, it is time for your last step: thinking about the consequences of these options. It sounds trivial, but most of the time when I get confronted with bad decisions I don't get a good answer to the question "What did you expect would happen?". Don't be that guy. Start thinking about how your scenarios will internally affect the people, the organization, the process and the IT. Try to cautiously talk to people internally who really know the system and the stakeholders about how they would expect a "hypothetical" scenario to go. But you really have to be careful, because people start talking fast and even just opening up the thought of a scenario may shift the political landscape drastically. Whenever you drop the word "lay-offs", you can be sure that people will get itchy.

After understanding of how your scenarios might affect the company itself, you should also try to understand how the scenarios will position the company in the market: are you moving yourself into a non-beneficial dependency in the value chain in the long run? Does it make the company more flexible if market circumstances change or do you get stuck? And lastly, you should reflect on how irreversible a decision is: can you switch later or do you have to commit now? How high are switching costs? When should a re-evaluation take place? Once you have thought of all of these questions, you are ready to decide.

Before we close off this section, I want to make one last warning: when you only see one option, you are the problem. There are always other options.

TO SUM THIS SECTION UP

Recommend a perspective, not an option. To think about options, first start thinking about what information you and/or your stakeholders need for a decision. Then make up three options that differ on the relevant dimensions. In the end think about the consequences these options have both inside the company and on the market position. Finish with thinking about how irreversible the different decision options are.

USE RESONATING PATTERNS

INSIGHT

During my consulting career, the concept of resonating patterns has led to a lot of my successes and accompanied me even through the most complicated client situations. And it is also one of the things that helped me in my private life in a significant way, therefore I hope that you may also gain a lot from understanding what I mean by these ominous "resonating patterns". Basically, this section gives you the insight on understanding people's reactions and how to make decisions in a way that uses their inherent energy. That sounds both very useful and quite ominous, doesn't it? So without lengthening this introduction, let's tackle this topic.

I would like to explore the general understanding of resonating patterns with you based on an example from physics that I am pretty sure you have already seen - at least in an animation movie. There you might have seen how someone makes a glass break by literally singing to it in the right pitch. What you witnessed is a phenomenon that piggybacks on the natural oscillation of an object. Every object has one. So, if you hit that natural oscillation with a corresponding energy from outside, your energy gets amplified by the object itself. Emitting this specific energy configuration is what I call a producing a resonating pattern.

This is where people come into the picture. People also have a natural oscillation. Hitting it, you can excite someone, which is somewhat of an equivalent to a glass bursting. Of course this is seldom the case with people when you hit a perfect high-pitched tone, but you have to understand it more from a cognitive point of view. People respond to ideas they like, thought patterns they deem reasonable and of course - other people they like. And just to give you a counter-example: Did you ever sit over lunch with somebody you did not have any connection with? You try starting a conversation about different topics, but your counterpart just does not respond or even seems lost - you are talking about the latest Coldplay album and your counterpart does not even care. Or your conversational partner starts telling you about the latest soccer results and you are just remarkably indifferent about it.

What can you make for yourself out of this nice, but until now pretty abstract idea, especially for the context of decision making? In general when you are preparing or making decisions, you try to come up with options that will further a goal. But the decision itself is just a stepping stone - the major work comes afterwards, be it a transformation of a sales organization or cutting costs in IT - and the overall success of an initiative gets measured afterwards based on the results of the work, not the decision. This means that a decision is worthless when people won't put in the work for it afterwards. And here you can see how our little concept of resonating patterns relates to making good decisions. You always want to decide so that you tap into the natural oscillation that powers the work that comes after. The power of this idea almost always wins versus an "objectively" better decision option - because it actually gets executed.

In order to tap into that inherent energy of other people you have to hit one of these natural oscillations by emitting some kind of resonating pattern. But how do you tap into the natural resonance and deliver those sweet resonating patterns? The answer is pretty basic: listen to people. They will tell you sooner or later what makes them tick, keeps them up at night and fascinates them. Listening is the key skill to understanding the wavelength of people and organizations. Moving on from there, try to evaluate:

What can you say that makes people's eyes shine?

Where do they instantly feel the need to say something?

Pay attention to how they react to you and adjust accordingly. Or in other words: don't talk about Coldplay when you notice that nobody cares. And when the time for decisions comes, try to keep natural oscillation in mind. The best part is: the same decision can either resonate with people or not - depending on how you frame and phrase it. Restructuring and letting go of a number of people does not really resonate with anyone. But thinking about how the future can be relatable for many people may.

Go out there and break some glasses!

TO SUM THIS SECTION UP

People and organizations have a natural oscillation that you can tap into by emitting a resonating pattern - be it a style of thinking, a topic or just being sympathetic. When making decisions, try to hit the natural oscillation in order to excite people for the path and therefore the chances of a successful decision.

SUMMARY OF SUMMARIES

CHAPTER 4: MAKE BETTER DECISIONS

1. **REALIZE THAT CHANGING SYSTEMS ARE NOT PRODUCTIVE**

   When advising management to take certain decisions, keep the resulting changes in mind and communicate them openly. Include the implications of change into your decision memos and thereby improve the decisions that are being made.

2. **BE CONFIDENT ABOUT WHAT YOU DO NOT KNOW**

   Do not expect yourself to know everything, but be very clear about the information you need for making a good decision possible. Focus on gathering the crucial information and be transparent about what you do not know. Decision making will improve if you are very clear about the required information.

3. **THINK IN FUTURE SCENARIOS**

   Think in scenarios. This includes defining what the relevant factors are that differentiate the three main scenarios and how you should act under those circumstances. Stop focusing on single numbers and think in meaningful ranges. Define a threshold for an exit scenario.

4. **CHALLENGE UNDERLYING BELIEFS**

Identify the existing belief systems within your project with regard to cause and effect, available options as well as desirable results in order to challenge them. This will improve decision making since you increase the options for actions, explore new business opportunities and therefore create greater impact.

5. **REFLECT ON DECISION OPTIONS**

Recommend a perspective, not an option. To think about options, first start thinking about what information you and/or your stakeholders need for a decision. Then make up three options that differ on the relevant dimensions. In the end think about the consequences these options have both inside the company and on the market position. Finish with thinking about how irreversible the different decision options are.

6. **USE RESONATING PATTERNS**

People and organizations have a natural oscillation that you can tap into by emitting a resonating pattern - be it a style of thinking, a topic or just being sympathetic. When making decisions, try to hit the natural oscillation in order to excite people for the path and therefore the chances of a successful decision.

TALKING ABOUT MAKING BETTER DECISIONS

Congratulations! You have definitely made the right decision by reading this book. We hope that we have delivered some impulses and that we contributed to making you more successful and bringing you closer to your goals. We selected the most relevant tactics and insights for everybody starting in the consulting industry. Together we turned the kaleidoscope of consulting 28 times and looked at this profession from different viewpoints. It is now up to you to use this knowledge to your advantage. Picking up this book every once in a while will give you a head start in the consulting business and will help you gain clarity with regard to your consulting career.

ACKNOWLEDGMENTS

Thank you to everyone who shared their insights and experiences with us. A special thanks to our families and friends who supported us putting this book together as well as everyone involved in improving the manuscript: Daniel Back, Heinz Janiec, Marvin Lamberjohann, Hans-Jürgen Moritz, Thorsten Poetzsch, Ann-Katrin Ripperger, Moritz Treutwein.

ABOUT THE AUTHORS

AXEL JANIEC

After studying business & economics in Mannheim and Bayreuth and working for an international logistics corporation, Axel started his career in consulting. Having worked on a wide range of projects in different industries and various countries he developed a holistic perspective on the way consulting works.

TRISTAN POETZSCH

The study of psychology in Wuerzburg quickly brought Tristan into the area of computer aided cognition, from where he started his journey into a career in consulting. The combination of informatics and human perspectives helped him develop a keen eye for socio-technological systems.

Axel and Tristan met on a consulting project. Their different approaches and perspectives on consulting and how to succeed in it triggered writing this book in a joined effort.

Printed in Poland
by Amazon Fulfillment
Poland Sp. z o.o., Wrocław

94256372R00080